LOGOS LATIN

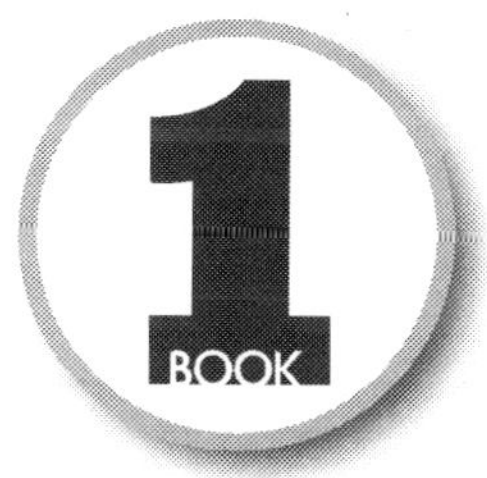

LOGOS LATIN

WRITTEN BY JULIE GARFIELD
ILLUSTRATED BY MARK BEAUCHAMP

LOGOS PRESS

Moscow, Idaho

Published by Logos Press, a division of Canon Press
PO Box 8729, Moscow, ID 83843
www.logospressonline.com
www.canonpress.com

Julie Garfield, *Logos Latin 1*

Revised 2012

Cover & page design by Lisa Beyeler
Illustrations by Mark Beauchamp

Printed in the United States of America

ISBN-13 978-1-935000-18-1
ISBN-10 1-935000-18-7

Table of Contents

UNIT FOUR

UNIT FIVE

STORIES

ACTIVITY PAGES

REFERENCE SECTION

GLOSSARY

Introduction

Welcome to LOGOS LATIN, BOOK 1. Latin is an ancient language which was spoken by the Romans. It continued to be spoken in Europe through the Middle Ages. Since then, students have studied Latin down to the present time.

You may not realize that you are already using Latin every day. Words like *solar, aquarium, glacier, dentist,* and *navy* are related to Latin words. In fact, about half of our English words have come from Latin. These words have made a long journey in terms of time and distance, traveling to us from ancient Rome, often detouring through France (or Italy or Spain) to England and finally reaching our shores. We call these English words *derivatives* and we will be spending a good amount of time discussing them.

While English vocabulary has been greatly influenced by Latin, it is not a direct descendent of Latin. On the other hand, Italian, French, Spanish, Portuguese, and Romanian, among others, are much more similar to Latin. You could say that Latin is the parent language and Italian, French, etc. are the children. These "children" are called *romance languages* because they are descended from the language of the Romans.

Learning Latin will also help us to better understand our own language. As we study Latin grammar we will make connections to English grammar. Latin is called an *inflected* language, which means that the endings change on words. The order of the words in a sentence is not as important in Latin as it is in English. It will be necessary to pay close attention to Latin word endings.

Studying Latin is like doing push-ups with your mind. It will strengthen your mental muscles, helping you to think carefully and practice accuracy. In a way, Latin is like math; all parts of the problem must be figured correctly. Latin will challenge you to do your very best.

As we begin our own Latin journey, I would like to introduce some friends who will be accompanying us through the pages of this book. Iulius, a Roman boy, and his sister, Iulia, will help us in our Latin study, as will their friend Saxum, a Roman rock we will be meeting a little later in the book.

Study diligently - learning Latin requires work. Exercise those minds! But also enjoy this very interesting language.

Vale,

Julie Garfield

Pronunciation & Grammar Guide

The following guide is based on the Classical pronunciation of Latin. In the Logos Latin 1 DVD, however, the letter *v* is pronounced as a "v" (not a "w") following Ecclesiastical Latin.

VOWELS

In Latin, vowels only have two pronunciations: long and short. In conversation, long vowels are held twice as long as short vowels. Long vowels are marked with a *macron* or line over the vowel (e.g., *ō*). Vowels without a macron are short vowels.

When spelling a word, including the macron is important in order to determine the meaning of the word.

Long Vowels

ā	like *a* in *water*:	**māter**
ē	like *eigh* in *weigh*:	**pēs**
ī	like *i* in *chlorine*:	**vīvo**
ō	like *o* in *hole*:	**creō**
ū	like *oo* in *food*:	**mūtō**

Short Vowels

a	like *a* in *fall*:	**caput**
e	like *e* in *red*:	**semper**
i	like *i* in *lick*:	**nihil**
o	like *o* in *Roman*:	**domus**
u	like *u* in *pull*:	**oculus**

DIPHTHONGS

When two vowel sounds are collapsed together into one syllable:

ae	like *y* in *style*:	**copiae**
au	like *ou* in *mouse*:	**audeo**
ei	like *ai* in *slain*:	**deinde**
eu	like *eew* in *Tuesday*:	**Orpheus**
oe	like *oi* in *spoil*:	**moenia**
ui	like *ew* in *stew*:	**huius**

CONSONANTS

Latin consonants are pronounced the same as English consonants with the following exceptions:

c	like *c* in *call*	never soft like *city, cell,* or *space*
g	like *g* in *golf*	never soft like *Germany, geography,* or *germ*
v	like *w* in *wow*	never like *vermin, victory,* or *varnish*
s	like *s* in *sister*	never like *easy, wise,* or *please*
ch	like *ch* in *chorus*	never like *chain, child,* or *chicken*
r	is trilled	like a cat purring
i	like *y* in *yes*	when used before a vowel at the beginning of a word or between two vowels within a word; at most other times it's used as a vowel

GRAMMAR ABBREVIATIONS

(as taught in Shurley English)

SN	Subject Noun
DO	Direct Object
IO	Indirect Object
PNA	Possessive Noun Adjective
OP	Object of Preposition
PrN	Predicate Noun
Adj	Adjective
V	Verb
V-t	Verb transitive
LV	Linking Verb
INF	Infinitive
Imp	Imperative (command)
Adv	Adverb
P	Preposition
C	Conjunction
C	Compound

(used in front of other abbreviations; CSN = Compound Subject Noun)

SENTENCE PATTERNS

The pattern of a sentence is the order of its main parts. The patterns taught at this level are:

SN V (P1)	subject noun, verb - pattern 1
SN V-t DO (P2)	subject noun, verb-transitive, direct object - pattern 2

Lesson One - The Very Beginning

A. VOCABULARY

Memorize the following Latin words and their meanings. A **translation** is the English meaning of a Latin word. On a piece of paper, practice writing each Latin word and its translation three times. Be sure to write the Latin word first and then the English.

We will also work together to write some derivatives on the blank lines. A **derivative** is an English word which comes from Latin. A derivative must be like the Latin word it comes from in two ways:

1. A derivative must be *similar* (like) in *spelling* to the Latin word.
2. A derivative must be *similar* (like) in *meaning* to the Latin word.

Your teacher will help you think of derivatives for the following words.

Word	Derivative	Translation
1. puer	____________________	*boy*
2. puella	____________________	*girl*
3. līberī	____________________	*children*

Est Iulia.

Est Iulius.

4. salvē ______________________ *hello (good day, be well)*

5. valē ______________________ *good bye (be well)*

6. amō ______________________ *I love*

7. est ______________________ *is* (also *"this is"*)

8. Quid est? ______________________ *What is it?*

9. Quis est? ______________________ *Who is it?*

10. et ______________________ *and*

B. VOCABULARY PRACTICE

Write the *Latin* for the following words. Be careful not to confuse the word *est* ("is") with the word *et* ("and")!

1. boy ______________________
2. girl ______________________
3. good day ______________________
4. good bye ______________________
5. I love ______________________
6. What is it? ______________________
7. is ______________________
8. Who is it? ______________________
9. and ______________________
10. children ______________________

C. DERIVATIVES

Underline the correct answer for the questions below:

Which derivative comes from the Latin word *amō*?

a) love b) amiable c) animal

Which derivative comes from the Latin word *salvē*?

a) servant b) dog c) salvation

D. VERB CHANT

Amō is a verb which means *I love.* By changing the endings on *amō* we can change the subject pronoun. Notice how the endings change in the chant below.

am**ō** - *I love*	am**āmus** - *we love*
am**ās** - *you love*	am**ātis** - *you all love*
am**at** - *he, she, it loves*	am**ant** - *they love*

What does *amō* mean? ______________________________

What does *amat* mean? ______________________________

How would you write *we love*? ______________________________

E. SAYING OF THE WEEK

Fide et amore (by faith and love)

Write the saying of the week and its meaning on the lines below.

Saying: ______________________________

Meaning: ______________________________

Lesson Two - Family

A. VOCABULARY

Memorize the following Latin words and their translations. On a piece of paper, practice writing each Latin word and its translation three times.

Word	Derivative	Translation
1. vir	____________________	*man*
2. fēmina	____________________	*woman*
3. pater	____________________	*father*
4. māter	____________________	*mother*
5. frāter	____________________	*brother*
6. soror	____________________	*sister*
7. familia	____________________	*family, household*
8. fīlius	____________________	*son*
9. fīlia	____________________	*daughter*
10. portō	____________________	*I carry*

B. VOCABULARY PRACTICE

Write the Latin for the following words.

1. son ______________________________
2. daughter ______________________________
3. family ______________________________
4. man ______________________________
5. mother ______________________________
6. I carry ______________________________
7. woman ______________________________
8. father ______________________________
9. brother ______________________________
10. sister ______________________________

C. DERIVATIVES

In a family, who shows *paternal* love? ______________________________

The word *paternal* comes from the Latin word ______________________________ .

Who shows *maternal* love? ______________________________

The word *maternal* comes from the Latin word ______________________________ .

If something is *portable*, you can ______________________________ it.

The word *portable* comes from the Latin word ______________________________ .

D. VERB CHANTS

Memorize the verb endings and meanings for the present tense.

-ō – *I*	-mus – *we*
-s – *you*	-tis – *you all*
-t – *he, she, it*	-nt – *they*

Where have you seen these endings before?

Now we will use these endings to conjugate the new verb, *portō.* To **conjugate** a verb means to change the endings. Highlight the endings on the Latin verbs and then highlight the English pronouns. The first one is done for you. Notice how the *-ō* is dropped off *portō* and the letter *-a* appears before the endings. This is called the **"A" Family or First Conjugation.**

portō - *I carry*	portāmus - *we carry*
portās - *you carry*	portātis - *you all carry*
portat - *he, she, it carries*	portant - *they carry*

E. SAYING OF THE WEEK

Vir sapit quī pauca loquitur (Wise is the man who talks little)

Write the saying of the week and its meaning on the lines below.

Saying: ______________________________

Meaning: ______________________________

F. REVIEW LIST

1. puer *boy*
2. puella *girl*
3. amō *I love*
4. salvē *hello (be well)*
5. valē *good bye (be well)*

Lesson Three - Home

A. VOCABULARY

Memorize the following words and their translations. On a piece of paper, practice writing each Latin word and its translation three times.

Word	Derivative	Translation
1. domus	______________________	*house, home*
2. ostium	______________________	*front door*
3. ātrium	______________________	*entrance room*
4. triclīnium	______________________	*dining room, dining couch*
5. cubiculum	______________________	*bedroom*
6. culīna	______________________	*kitchen*
7. mensa	______________________	*table, desk*
8. sella	______________________	*seat, chair*
9. lectus	______________________	*bed*
10. solum	______________________	*floor*
11. tectum	______________________	*ceiling, roof*
12. lucerna	______________________	*lamp*
13. sedeō	______________________	*I sit*
14. dormiō	______________________	*I sleep*
15. habitō	______________________	*I live in*

B. VOCABULARY PRACTICE

Write the Latin for the following words:

1. house, home ______________________
2. front door ______________________
3. I live in ______________________
4. I sleep ______________________
5. entrance room ______________________
6. dining room, dining couch ______________________
7. I sit ______________________
8. lamp ______________________
9. bedroom ______________________
10. kitchen ______________________
11. table, desk ______________________
12. seat, chair ______________________
13. ceiling, roof ______________________
14. floor ______________________
15. bed ______________________

Quid est?
Est ______________

Quid est?
Est ______________

C. DERIVATIVES

Give the Latin word from which each of these derivatives comes.

1. The English word *dormitory* comes from the Latin word ______________________________ .
2. The English word *habitat* comes from the Latin word ______________________________ .
3. The English word *domestic* comes from the Latin word ______________________________ .

Underline the correct word in the sentences below.

1. In a *dormitory* people : a) eat b) sleep c) exercise
2. A *habitat* for ducks would be: a) a desert b) a mountain c) a pond
3. *Domestic* chores are chores you do: a) at school b) at the park c) at home

D. VERB CHANTS

Write in the meanings for the present tense verb endings:

-ō –	-mus –
-s –	-tis –
-t –	-nt –

Use the present tense endings above to conjugate (put endings on) the verb *habitō* and then translate (give meanings) for all its forms.

habitō – *I live in*	

Now translate these forms of *habitō* and *amō*. Underline endings.

1. habitās ______________________________
2. amāmus ______________________________
3. habitāmus ______________________________
4. amant ______________________________
5. habitātis ______________________________
6. amat ______________________________
7. habitō ______________________________

E. SAYING OF THE WEEK

Festīnā lente (Make haste slowly)

Write the saying and its meaning on the lines:

Saying: ____

Meaning: ____

F. REVIEW LIST

1. fīlius	*son*
2. frāter	*brother*
3. fīlia	*daughter*
4. soror	*sister*
5. portō	*I carry*
6. pater	*father*
7. māter	*mother*

Shh... Iulius dormit. (Julius is sleeping.)

Lesson Four - School

A. VOCABULARY

Memorize the following words and their translations. On a piece of paper, practice writing each Latin word and its translation three times.

Word	Derivative	Translation
1. lūdus	______________________	*school, game*
2. schola	______________________	*class, classroom*
3. discipulus	______________________	*boy student*
4. discipula	______________________	*girl student*
5. magister	______________________	*male teacher*
6. magistra	______________________	*female teacher*
7. tabula	______________________	*board, tablet*
8. liber	______________________	*book*
9. charta	______________________	*piece of paper*
10. stylus	______________________	*pencil*
11. laudō	______________________	*I praise*
12. rogō	______________________	*I ask*
13. respondeō	______________________	*I answer*
14. bonus	______________________	*good*
15. malus	______________________	*bad*

B. VOCABULARY PRACTICE

Write the Latin for the following words:

1. I praise ______________________
2. good ______________________
3. I ask ______________________
4. pencil ______________________
5. male teacher ______________________
6. boy student ______________________
7. piece of paper ______________________
8. class, classroom ______________________
9. school ______________________
10. board ______________________
11. girl student ______________________
12. female teacher ______________________
13. book ______________________
14. I answer ______________________
15. bad ______________________

C. DERIVATIVES

For each of the following English *derivatives* underline the correct Latin word it comes from:

1. A *disciple* is a student of religion or learning. In the New Testament, a disciple is a follower of Jesus. *Disciple* comes from the Latin word:

   a) bonus   b) respondeō   c) discipulus

2. A *tablet* is a writing pad made of pieces of paper glued together at one edge. *Tablet* comes from the Latin word:

   a) magister   b) tabula   c) charta

3. An *interrogative* sentence asks a question. *Interrogative* comes from the Latin word:

   a) respondeō   b) rogō   c) stylus

D. VERBS

There are five **helping verbs** for the present tense - *am*, *is*, *are*, *do*, and *does*. You already know the present tense endings and meanings but we can also translate these endings using helping verbs. The present tense can be translated in three different ways:

1. No helping verb
2. Use one of these helping verbs: *am, is, are*
3. Use one of these helping verbs: *do, does*

Now translate forms of *amō* in three ways. The first two are done for you.

1. amō - I love, I am loving, I do love

2. amās - you love, you are loving, you do love

3. amat - ______________________, ______________________,
____

4. amāmus - ______________________, ______________________,
____

5. amātis - ______________________, ______________________,
____

6. amant - ______________________, ______________________,
____

More Verb Practice - Conjugate and translate *rogō*:

rogō -	

E. TRANSLATION

Translate the following verbs from Lists 1, 2, and 3. Underline endings.

1. amant ____________________
2. habitō ____________________
3. portātis ____________________
4. rogāmus ____________________
5. portās ____________________
6. rogat ____________________

F. SAYING OF THE WEEK

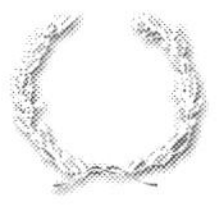

Ex librīs (From the books of)

Write the saying and its meaning on the lines:

Saying ____________________

Meaning ____________________

G. REVIEW LIST

1. culīna	*kitchen*
2. triclīnium	*dining room*
3. tectum	*ceiling, roof*
4. solum	*floor*
5. domus	*house, home*
6. lectus	*bed*
7. sedeō	*I sit*
8. dormiō	*I sleep*
9. Quid est?	*What is it?*
10 Quis est?	*Who is it?*

Lesson Five - City

A. VOCABULARY

Memorize the following words and their translations. On a piece of paper, practice writing each Latin word and its translation three times.

Word	Derivative	Translation
1. urbs	______________________	*city*
2. oppidum	______________________	*town*
3. vicus	______________________	*village*
4. cīvis	______________________	*citizen*
5. populus	______________________	*people, nation*
6. turba	______________________	*crowd*
7. via	______________________	*road, way*
8. forum	______________________	*marketplace, public square*
9. taberna	______________________	*shop*
10. pistrīnum	______________________	*bakery*
11. pecūnia	______________________	*money*
12. Rōma	______________________	*Rome*
13. aedificium	______________________	*building*
14. ambulō	______________________	*I walk*
15. spectō	______________________	*I look at, watch*

B. VOCABULARY PRACTICE

Write the Latin for the following words:

1. I look at ______________________________
2. building ______________________________
3. bakery ______________________________
4. shop ______________________________
5. road, way ______________________________
6. people, nation ______________________________
7. village ______________________________
8. city ______________________________
9. I walk ______________________________
10. Rome ______________________________
11. money ______________________________
12. marketplace ______________________________
13. crowd ______________________________
14. citizen ______________________________
15. town ______________________________

C. DERIVATIVES

Find the mystery derivative!

Below are three Latin words and clues. Try to give the derivative. Remember that a derivative has a similar spelling and a similar meaning to the Latin word.

1. *spectō* - This derivative is another name for eye glasses.

   What is it? ______________________________

2. *ambulō* - This derivative is a type of van that carries people who are too sick or injured to walk.

   What is it? ______________________________

3. *populus* - This derivative describes someone who is well liked by many people. What is it?

   What is it? ______________________________

D. VERB CHANTS

Memorize the **Linking Verb Chant** and its meanings:

LINKING VERB (PRESENT TENSE)

sum - *I am*	sumus - *we are*
es - *you are*	estis - *you all are*
est - *he, she, it is*	sunt - *they are*

Practice writing the new chant and its meanings in the box below:

E. HELPING VERBS

In Lesson 4 we learned the five helping verbs for the present tense. Fill in the missing helping verbs on the blanks below:

1. am______ 2. ________ 3. ________ 4. do______ 5. ________

Present tense verbs (those that end with *ō, s, t, mus, tis, nt*) can be translated in three ways. Study the example below and then translate *ambulāmus* in three ways.

Example: **ambulās** - *1. you walk 2. you are walking 3. you do walk*

ambulāmus - 1. ________________ 2. ________________ 3. ________________

F. TRANSLATION

Translate the following verbs and <u>underline</u> endings:

1. rogātis ____________________
2. spectās ____________________
3. habitō ____________________
4. ambulant ____________________
5. portat ____________________
6. amāmus ____________________

G. SAYING OF THE WEEK

Quid est?
Est ____________

Vox populī (the voice of the people)

Write the saying and its meaning on the lines below.

Saying: ____

Meaning: ____

H. REVIEW LIST

1. lūdus	*school*	6. ostium	*front door*
2. schola	*class, classroom*	7. ātrium	*entrance room*
3. liber	*book*	8. mensa	*table, desk*
4. tabula	*board, tablet*	9. vir	*man*
5. rogō	*I ask*	10. fēmina	*woman*

Lesson Six - Farm

A. VOCABULARY

Memorize the following words and their translations. On a piece of paper, practice writing each Latin word and its translation three times.

Word	Derivative	Translation
1. agricola	____________	*farmer*
2. ager	____________	*field*
3. villa	____________	*farmhouse*
4. equus	____________	*horse*
5. bōs	____________	*cow, bull*
6. gallus	____________	*rooster*
7. gallīna	____________	*hen*
8. ōvum	____________	*egg*
9. porcus	____________	*pig*
10. stabulum	____________	*stable*
11. pastor	____________	*shepherd*
12. ovis	____________	*sheep*
13. vigilō	____________	*I guard*
14. arō	____________	*I plow*
15. labōrō	____________	*I work*

B. VOCABULARY PRACTICE

Write the Latin for the following words:

1. I plow ______________________________
2. sheep ______________________________
3. stable ______________________________
4. egg ______________________________
5. rooster ______________________________
6. horse ______________________________
7. field ______________________________
8. farmer ______________________________
9. farmhouse ______________________________
10. cow ______________________________
11. hen ______________________________
12. pig ______________________________
13. shepherd ______________________________
14. I guard ______________________________
15. I work ______________________________

C. DERIVATIVES

Equine, bovine, ovine, and *porcine* are English derivatives which describe certain animals. First in Latin and then in English, tell what animal is being described:

	LATIN	ENGLISH
porcine -	______________________	______________________
ovine -	______________________	______________________
equine -	______________________	______________________
bovine -	______________________	______________________

The English word *oval* comes from the Latin word *ōvum*. If something is *oval*, it is shaped like an__________

D. VERB CHANTS

Memorize the Future Tense Verb Chant and its meanings. Do you recognize a pattern from another chant we've learned?

FUTURE TENSE VERB ENDINGS

-bō – *I will*	-bimus – *we will*
-bis – *you will*	-bitis – *you all will*
-bit – *he, she, it will*	-bunt – *they will*

Now practice writing the new chant and its meanings in the box below:

E. FUTURE TENSE VERBS

Study the following examples of future tense verbs. Underline the endings and the helping verbs.

arābō - I will plow *labōrābunt* - they will work *vigilābit* - he will guard

Now underline the endings on the verbs below and translate. They are all in the future tense.

1. labōrābō ______________________________
2. arābit ______________________________
3. vigilābimus ______________________________
4. vigilābunt ______________________________
5. arābis ______________________________
6. labōrābitis ______________________________

F. SAYING OF THE WEEK

Labor omnia vincit (Work conquers all)

This is the motto of Oklahoma.

Write the saying of the week and its meaning below.

Saying: ____

Meaning: ____

G. REVIEW LIST

1. urbs — *city*
2. oppidum — *town*
3. cīvis — *citizen*
4. via — *road, way*
5. ambulō — *I walk*
6. spectō — *I look at*
7. discipula — *girl student*
8. magister — *male teacher*
9. taberna — *shop*
10. habitō — *I live in*

Unit One Review - Lessons 1 through 6

A. VOCABULARY (Latin to English)

Study Lists 1 - 6 for three to five minutes. Without looking, write down the English meanings for as many of the following words as you can remember. Finally, check your answers by looking back through Lists 1 - 6. Use a red pen to write in the correct answers of those you missed or left blank.

1. puer ____________________
2. frāter ____________________
3. familia ____________________
4. vigilō ____________________
5. equus ____________________
6. cubiculum ____________________
7. lectus ____________________
8. sedeō ____________________
9. schola ____________________
10. magistra ____________________
11. stylus ____________________
12. aedificium ____________________
13. via ____________________
14. vir ____________________
15. pater ____________________
16. labōrō ____________________
17. agricola ____________________
18. ōvum ____________________
19. mensa ____________________
20. tectum ____________________
21. cīvis ____________________
22. discipula ____________________
23. liber ____________________
24. taberna ____________________
25. spectō ____________________

B. VOCABULARY (English to Latin)

Study Lists 1 - 6 for three to five minutes. This time look at the English word first and then look at its Latin form. From memory, write as many of the *Latin* words as you can remember. Don't worry too much about spelling. When you are finished, look up the ones you don't remember and write the correct answers using a red pen.

1. I plow ______________________
2. pig ______________________
3. field ______________________
4. people, nation ______________________
5. marketplace ______________________
6. good ______________________
7. I praise ______________________
8. school ______________________
9. kitchen ______________________
10. floor ______________________
11. girl ______________________
12. sister ______________________
13. I love ______________________
14. sheep ______________________
15. cow ______________________
16. city ______________________
17. I walk ______________________
18. Rome ______________________
19. I answer ______________________
20. piece of paper ______________________
21. dining room ______________________
22. I sleep ______________________
23. house ______________________
24. woman ______________________
25. mother ______________________

C. DERIVATIVES

Here are some English derivatives. Write the Latin word each one comes from on the blanks.

1. *maternal* - ______________________
2. *paternal* - ______________________

3. *portable* - ______________________________

4. *dormitory* - ______________________________

5. *habitat* - ______________________________

6. *domestic* - ______________________________

7. *disciple* - ______________________________

8. *tablet* - ______________________________

9. *interrogative* - ______________________________

10. *spectacles* - ______________________________

11. *ambulance* - ______________________________

12. *popular* - ______________________________

13. *porcine* - ______________________________

14. *ovine* - ______________________________

15. *bovine* - ______________________________

16. *equine* - ______________________________

17. *oval* - ______________________________

Now choose one *derivative,* look it up in an *English* dictionary, and write the word and its meaning below:

Word ______________________________

Meaning ____

____

D. VERB CHANTS

Fill in the following verb chants and meanings. Do as much as you can from memory and then look up any you are not sure of:

AMŌ CHANT - FIRST CONJUGATION

amō –	

PRESENT TENSE VERB ENDINGS

-ō –	

LINKING VERB (PRESENST TENSE)

sum –	

FUTURE TENSE VERB ENDINGS

-bō –	

E. TRANSLATION

Now translate the following verbs. Underline endings!

1. amat ____________________
2. portāmus ____________________
3. amābit ____________________
4. portābimus ____________________

5. habitās ______	6. rogābunt ______
7. habitābis ______	8. rogō ______
9. spectābō ______	10. ambulant ______
11. arābitis ______	12. labōrat ______

F. SAYINGS OF THE WEEK

Translate the sayings we have learned so far:

1. *Fide et amore* ______

2. *Festinā lente* ______

3. *Ex librīs* ______

4. *Vox populī* ______

5. *Labor omnia vincit* ______

   This is the motto for what state? ______

6. *Vir sapit quī pauca loquitur* ______

Lesson Seven - Outdoors

A. VOCABULARY

Memorize the following words and their translations. On a piece of paper, practice writing each Latin word and its translation three times.

Word	Derivative	Translation
1. āēr	______________________	*air*
2. terra	______________________	*land, earth*
3. campus	______________________	*plain, level area*
4. saxum	______________________	*rock*
5. silva	______________________	*forest*
6. arbor	______________________	*tree*
7. mōns	______________________	*mountain*
8. fluvius	______________________	*river*
9. lacus	______________________	*lake*
10. oceanus	______________________	*ocean*
11. harēna	______________________	*beach, sand*
12. insula	______________________	*island*
13. aqua	______________________	*water*
14. nō	______________________	*I swim*
15. explōrō	______________________	*I explore*

B. VOCABULARY PRACTICE

Salve!
Sum Saxum.

Write the Latin for the following words:

1. I explore ____________________
2. island ____________________
3. ocean ____________________
4. river ____________________
5. tree ____________________
6. rock ____________________
7. land, earth ____________________
8. air ____________________
9. plain, level area ____________________
10. forest ____________________
11. mountain ____________________
12. lake ____________________
13. beach, sand ____________________
14. I swim ____________________
15. water ____________________

C. DERIVATIVES

Look up these derivatives in an English dictionary and give their definitions (meanings).

1. A *peninsula* is ____

____

What Latin word does *peninsula* come from? ____________________

What state in the United States is a very large peninsula? ____________________

2. *Sylvan* means ____

____

What Latin word does *sylvan* come from? ____________________

3. An *arboretum* is ____

What Latin word does *arboretum* come from? ____________________

D. CONJUGATION

Conjugate (put endings on) and translate (give meanings) for the linking verb.

LINKING VERB (PRESENT TENSE)

sum -	

Quid est?

Est ____________

Study the examples and then translate the sentences below:

Sum magistra. - *I am a female teacher.* Es puer. - *You are a boy.* Est saxum. - *It is a rock.*

1. Sum agricola. ______________________________

2. Es discipula. ______________________________

3. Est ōvum. ______________________________

E. CONJUGATION & TRANSLATION

Conjugate and translate explōrō in the present and future tenses in the boxes below:

PRESENT TENSE VERB ENDINGS

explōrō - *I explore*	

FUTURE TENSE VERB ENDING

explōrābō - *I will explore*	

Now underline the endings on the following verbs and translate. Some are present tense and some are future tense.

1. nō ____________________ 2. nābit ____________________

3. ambulābunt ____________________ 4. vigilāmus ____________________

5. respondēbis ____________________ 6. amātis ____________________

F. SAYING OF THE WEEK

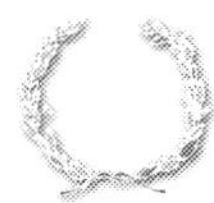

Montanī semper līberī (Mountaineers are always free)

This is the motto of West Virginia.

Write the saying of the week and its meaning below.

Saying: ____

Meaning: ____

G. REVIEW LIST

1. agricola *farmer*
2. ager *field*
3. arō *I plow*
4. villa *farmhouse*
5. vicus *village*
6. pistrīnum *bakery*
7. sella *seat, chair*
8. forum *marketplace, public square*
9. charta *piece of paper*
10. cubiculum *bedroom*
11. ambulō *I walk*
12. vigilō *I guard*

Quid est?

Est ______________

Lesson Eight - Animals

A. VOCABULARY

Memorize the following words and their translations. On a piece of paper, practice writing each Latin word and its translation three times.

Word	Derivative	Translation
1. animal	__________	*animal*
2. lupus	__________	*wolf*
3. ursus	__________	*bear*
4. cunīculus	__________	*rabbit*
5. rāna	__________	*frog*
6. sciūrus	__________	*squirrel*
7. cervus	__________	*deer*
8. canis	__________	*dog*
9. fēles	__________	*cat*
10. spēlunca	__________	*cave*
11. stagnum	__________	*pond*
12. ululō	__________	*I howl*
13. videō	__________	*I see*
14. terreō	__________	*I frighten*
15. timeō	__________	*I fear*

B. VOCABULARY PRACTICE

Write the Latin for the following words:

1. wolf ______________________
2. I frighten ______________________
3. bear ______________________
4. cat ______________________
5. pond ______________________
6. rabbit ______________________
7. frog ______________________
8. squirrel ______________________
9. dog ______________________
10. I fear ______________________
11. cave ______________________
12. deer ______________________
13. I howl ______________________
14. animal ______________________
15. I see ______________________

C. DERIVATIVES

<u>Underline</u> the correct choice for each sentence.

1. If a wolf *terrifies* a squirrel, he:
   a) eats it. b) frightens it. c) chases it.

2. If a deer is *timid* of a bear, it is:
   a) afraid. b) charging the bear. c) sleeping.

3. What animal would eat *canine* food?
   a) A squirrel b) A frog. c) A dog.

4. What do you call someone who likes to explore caves?
   a) Stagnant. b) A spelunker. c) A feline.

5. What animal is sometimes called a *coney*?
   a) A dog. b) A rabbit. c) A cat.

D. VERB CHANT

Here is a new chant to learn. *Videō* represents the "E" Family of verbs which is called **Second Conjugation.** Second conjugation (or "E" Family) verbs use the same endings as first conjugation ("A" Family) verbs, but an *e* appears before the endings instead of an *a*.

Study and memorize the *Videō* Chant below. Highlight the *e* before each ending.

VIDEŌ CHANT - SECOND CONJUGATION (in the present tense)

videō - *I see*	vidēmus - *we see*
vidēs - *you see*	vidētis - *you all see*
videt - *he, she, it sees*	vident - *they see*

Practice writing the *Videō* Chant and its meanings:

Now study *videō* in the future. Highlight the *e* before each future tense ending.

VIDEŌ CHANT - SECOND CONJUGATION (in the future tense)

vidēbō - *I will see*	vidēbimus - *we will see*
vidēbis - *you will see*	vidēbitis - *you all will see*
vidēbit - *he, she, it will see*	vidēbunt - *they will see*

E. PRESENT & FUTURE TENSE PRACTICE

Below are some verbs with present and future tense endings. Underline the endings and translate the verbs. Circle verbs from the second conjugation. The first one is done for you.

1. terrēbis you will frighten
2. respondent ____________
3. amat ____________
4. vidēs ____________
5. explōrābunt ____________
6. terrēmus ____________
7. timētis ____________
8. vidēbimus ____________
9. terreō ____________
10. ululābit ____________
11. timēbō ____________
12. ululābitis ____________

F. SAYING OF THE WEEK

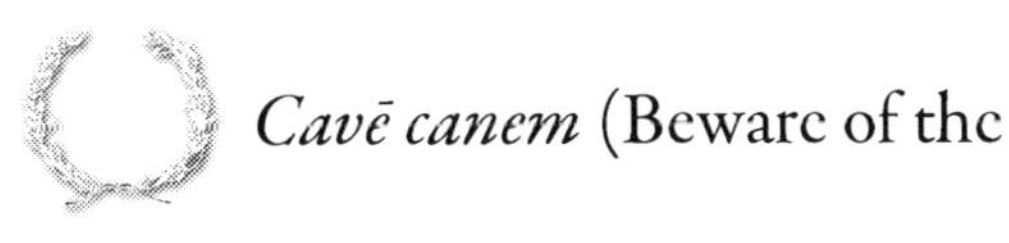

Cavē canem (Beware of the dog)

Write the saying of the week and its meaning below.

Saying: ____________________

Meaning: ____________________

Draw a dog house and a sign with *cavē canem* on it. Feel free to put a *canis* in the picture.

Some Roman dogs had the name *Fido,* which comes from the Latin word *fidus* (faithful). *Ferox* was another Roman dog name. If you have extra time, look up the word *ferox* in a Latin dictionary and write its meaning on the line below.

Ferox means ______________________________

G. REVIEW LIST

1. terra — *land, earth*
2. mōns — *mountain*
3. porcus — *pig*
4. gallīna — *hen*
5. ovis — *sheep*
6. equus — *horse*
7. insula — *island*
8. lacus — *lake*
9. bonus — *good*
10. vigilō — *I guard*

Lesson Nine - Fish and Birds

A. VOCABULARY

Memorize the following words and their translations. On a piece of paper, practice writing each Latin word and its translation three times.

Word	Derivative	Translation
1. piscis	__________	*fish*
2. delphīnus	__________	*dolphin*
3. orca	__________	*whale*
4. cancer	__________	*crab*
5. avis	__________	*bird*
6. columba	__________	*dove, pigeon*
7. strix	__________	*owl*
8. aquila	__________	*eagle*
9. āla	__________	*wing*
10. pinna	__________	*feather*
11. nīdus	__________	*nest*
12. scopulus	__________	*cliff, rock formation*
13. cantō	__________	*I sing*
14. volō	__________	*I fly*
15. habeō	__________	*I have or hold*

B. VOCABULARY PRACTICE

Write the Latin for the following words:

1. I fly ______________________________
2. nest ______________________________
3. feather ______________________________
4. eagle ______________________________
5. dove, pigeon ______________________________
6. crab ______________________________
7. dolphin ______________________________
8. fish ______________________________
9. whale ______________________________
10. bird ______________________________
11. owl ______________________________
12. wing ______________________________
13. cliff ______________________________
14. I sing ______________________________
15. I have or hold ______________________________

C. DERIVATIVES

Look up the *italicized* derivatives in an English dictionary and fill in the blanks. Also tell the Latin origin.

1. What animal might live in an *aviary*? ______________________________

   Latin origin for *aviary*? ______________________________

2. If a person has an *aquiline* nose, he has a nose like what animal? ______________________________

   Latin origin for *aquiline*? ______________________________

Challenge Question! A very famous gigantic *sculpture* carved directly into a mountain rock formation pictures four American presidents: George Washington, Thomas Jefferson, Abraham Lincoln, and Theodore Roosevelt. In what state can you see this sculpture?

____

Latin origin for *sculpture*? ______________________________

D. VERB CHANT

Learn the new verb chant below. This chant is called the **Imperfect Tense Chant** and it refers to actions which happened in the past. Look for familiar patterns.

IMPERFECT TENSE VERB ENDINGS

-bam – *I was*	-bāmus - *we were*
-bās - *you were*	-bātis - *you all were*
-bat - *he, she, it was*	-bant - *they were*

Quid est?

Est ______________

Practice writing the imperfect tense chant and meanings:

Translate the following verbs containing imperfect tense endings. Underline endings.

1. cantābam ______________________
2. habēbant ______________________
3. cantābātis ______________________
4. habēbāmus ______________________
5. cantābās ______________________
6. habēbat ______________________

Quid est?

Est ______________

E. TRANSLATION

Now translate these verbs which contain present, future, and imperfect tense endings. Underline endings. Highlight the **vowel** before each verb ending. Verbs are from Lists 8 and 9.

1. terrēbunt ______________________
2. timēbant ______________________
3. vidēbis ______________________
4. volābat ______________________
5. cantābit ______________________
6. habēmus ______________________
7. ululābam ______________________
8. cantābō ______________________
9. habētis ______________________
10. terrēbās ______________________

F. SAYING OF THE WEEK

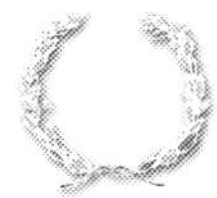 *Piscem natāre docēre* (to teach a fish to swim)

Write the saying of the week and its meaning below.

Saying: ______________________________

Meaning: ______________________________

G. REVIEW LIST

1. terreō — *I frighten*
2. labōrō — *I work*
3. canis — *dog*
4. fēles — *cat*
5. lupus — *wolf*
6. stagnum — *pond*
7. oceanus — *ocean*
8. explōrō — *I explore*
9. populus — *people, nation*
10. laudō — *I praise*

Lesson Ten - The Heavens

A. VOCABULARY

Memorize the following words and their translations. On a piece of paper, practice writing each word and its translation three times.

Word	Derivative	Translation
1. caelum	______________	*sky, heaven*
2. sōl	______________	*sun*
3. lūna	______________	*moon*
4. nimbus	______________	*storm cloud*
5. stella	______________	*star*
6. astrum	______________	*constellation*
7. sagittārius	______________	*archer*
8. aquārius	______________	*water-carrier*
9. scorpius	______________	*scorpion*
10. geminus	______________	*twin*
11. lībra	______________	*pair of scales*
12. vaga	______________	*planet*
13. diēs	______________	*day*
14. nox	______________	*night*
15. lūceō	______________	*I shine*

B. VOCABULARY PRACTICE

Write the Latin for the following words:

1. sky, heaven ______________________
2. cloud ______________________
3. water-carrier ______________________
4. planet ______________________
5. sun ______________________
6. constellation ______________________
7. twin ______________________
8. night ______________________
9. moon ______________________
10. archer ______________________
11. pair of scales ______________________
12. I shine ______________________
13. star ______________________
14. scorpion ______________________
15. day ______________________

Quid est?

Est ______________

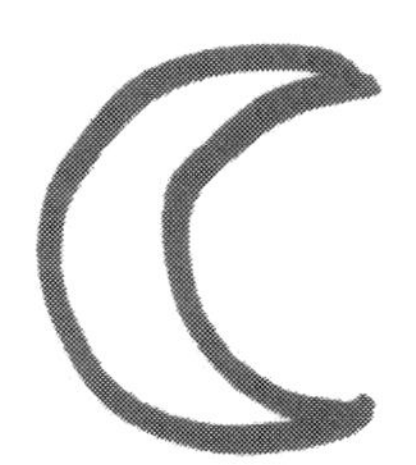

Quid est?

Est ______________

C. DERIVATIVES

Fill in the blanks about these derivatives. Tell the Latin word each derivative comes from.

1. When someone studies *astronomy*, he is studying the ______________________________.

    Latin word ______________________________

2. When something is *diurnal,* it happens during the ______________________________.

    Latin word ______________________________

3. If an animal is *nocturnal,* when does it hunt for food? ______________________________

    Latin word ______________________________

4. *Solar* energy comes from the ______________________________.

    Latin word ______________________________

5. If an astronaut makes a *lunar* landing, he has landed on the ______________________________.

    Latin word ______________________________

D. VERB CHANTS

Memorize the following chant. Do you recognize a pattern? Highlight the parts you have seen before.

POSSUM CHANT

possum - *I am able*	possumus - *we are able*
potes - *you are able*	potestis - *you all are able*
potest - *he, she, it is able*	possunt - *they are able*

Now practice writing the new chant and its meanings.

E. VERB REVIEW

Translate these sentences containing forms of the linking verb *sum.*

1. Sum aquārius. ______________________

2. Est cancer. ______________________

3. Es sagittārius. ______________________

Now practice translating verbs from the present, future, and imperfect tenses. <u>Underline</u> endings.

1. lūcet ______________________

   lūcēbit ______________________

   lūcēbat ______________________

2. volābō ______________________

   volō ______________________

   volābam ______________________

3. cantābāmus ______________________

   cantābimus ______________________

   cantāmus ______________________

4. vidētis ______________________

vidēbitis ______________________

vidēbātis ______________________

5. terrēbās ______________________

terrēbis ______________________

terrēs ______________________

6. ululant ______________________

ululābunt ______________________

ululābant ______________________

F. SAYING OF THE WEEK

Sōl lūcet omnibus (the sun shines on all)

Write the saying of the week and its meaning below.

Saying: ______________________________________

Meaning: ______________________________________

G. REVIEW LIST

1. piscis — *fish*
2. cancer — *crab*
3. aquila — *eagle*
4. delphīnus — *dolphin*
5. columba — *dove*
6. ursus — *bear*
7. avis — *bird*
8. aqua — *water*
9. harēna — *beach, sand*
10. volō — *I fly*

Lesson Eleven - Weather

A. VOCABULARY

Memorize the following words and their translations. On a piece of paper, practice writing each word and its translation.

Word	Derivative	Translation
1. tempestās	__________	*weather, storm*
2. ventus	__________	*wind*
3. imber	__________	*rain*
4. nix	__________	*snow*
5. glaciēs	__________	*ice*
6. nūbes	__________	*cloud*
7. umbra	__________	*shadow, shade*
8. fulgur	__________	*lightning*
9. tonitrus	__________	*thunder*
10. arcus pluvius	__________	*rainbow*
11. flō	__________	*I blow*
12. pluit	__________	*it's raining*
13. ningit	__________	*it's snowing*
14. calidus	__________	*hot*
15. gelidus	__________	*cold*

B. VOCABULARY PRACTICE

Write the Latin for the following words:

1. hot ____________________
2. it's raining ____________________
3. rainbow ____________________
4. lightning ____________________
5. cloud ____________________
6. snow ____________________
7. wind ____________________
8. weather, storm ____________________
9. rain ____________________
10. ice ____________________
11. shadow, shade ____________________
12. thunder ____________________
13. I blow ____________________
14. it's snowing ____________________
15. cold ____________________

C. DERIVATIVES

Underline the correct choice for each sentence.

1. A *glacier* is made of: a) rain b) clouds c) ice

2. A *tempest* is: a) a very bad storm b) a temper tantrum c) a snake

3. On a *niveous* day it is: a) sunny b) snowy c) windy

Now fill in the blanks below:

At the beach, people sometimes use an ______________________ for shade.

Challenge Question!

If a roof has shingles arranged in an *imbricate* pattern, the shingles look like ______________.

D. VERB CHANTS

Here is a new chant to learn. It is called the **Perfect Tense Chant.** Do you recognize a pattern we have seen before?

PERFECT TENSE VERB ENDINGS

-ī	-imus
-istī	-istis
-it	-ērunt

Practice writing the new chant. You do not have to know the meanings for this one.

E. TRANSLATION

Translate *flō*, the only verb from List 11, and underline endings. Remember that the *o* changes to an *a* before the endings because *flō* is a First Conjugation, or "A" Family verb.

1. flābunt ______________________
2. flās ______________________
3. flābam ______________________
4. flābit ______________________
5. flābās ______________________
6. flābat ______________________
7. flābitis ______________________
8. flātis ______________________
9. flābāmus ______________________
10. flant ______________________
11. flābātis ______________________
12. flō ______________________
13. flāmus ______________________
14. flābimus ______________________
15. flābō ______________________
16. flat ______________________
17. flābis ______________________
18. flābant ______________________

F. SAYING OF THE WEEK

In principiō creāvit Deus caelum et terram (In the beginning God created the heavens and the earth. Genesis 1:1)

Write the saying of the week and its meaning below.

Saying: ____

Meaning: ____

G. REVIEW LIST

1. sōl — *sun*
2. nimbus — *storm cloud*
3. diēs — *day*
4. nox — *night*
5. scopulus — *cliff, rock formation*
6. silva — *forest*
7. spēlunca — *cave*
8. sciūrus — *squirrel*
9. lūcēo — *I shine*
10. habeō — *I have or hold*

Unit Two Review - Lessons 7 through 11

A. VOCABULARY (Latin to English)

Study Lists 7 - 11 for three to five minutes. Without looking, write down the English meanings for as many of the following words as you can remember. Finally, check your answers by looking back through Lists 7 - 11. Use a red pen to write in the correct answers of those you missed or left blank.

1. āēr ______________________
2. fluvius ______________________
3. insula ______________________
4. canis ______________________
5. videō ______________________
6. habeō ______________________
7. avis ______________________
8. aquila ______________________
9. vaga ______________________
10. nox ______________________
11. tempestās ______________________
12. flō ______________________
13. umbra ______________________
14. arbor ______________________
15. harēna ______________________
16. ursus ______________________
17. spēlunca ______________________
18. cunīculus ______________________
19. volō ______________________
20. orca ______________________
21. astrum ______________________
22. lūna ______________________
23. lūceō ______________________
24. ventus ______________________
25. glaciēs ______________________

B. VOCABULARY (English to Latin)

Study Lists 7 - 11 for three to five minutes, but this time look at the *English* word first, and then at its Latin meaning. From memory, write as many of the *Latin* words as you can remember. Don't worry too much about spelling. When you are finished, look up the ones you don't remember and write the correct answers using a red pen.

1. plain, level area ________________	14. forest ________________
2. mountain ________________	15. I swim________________
3. land, earth ________________	16. I fear ________________
4. pond ________________	17. wolf ________________
5. frog ________________	18. I frighten ________________
6. fish ________________	19. dolphin ________________
7. dove, pigeon ________________	20. wing ________________
8. crab ________________	21. sun ________________
9. star ________________	22. water-carrier ________________
10. sky, heaven ________________	23. cloud ________________
11. snow ________________	24. rain ________________
12. thunder ________________	25. it's raining ________________
13. cold ________________	

C. DERIVATIVES

Write the letter of the correct Latin origin* on the blank next to these derivatives from Lists 7 - 11:

DERIVATIVES	LATIN ORIGIN
1. ______ glacier	A. *astrum*
2. ______ sculpture	B. *avis*
3. ______ canine	C. *terreō*
4. ______ peninsula	D. *glaciēs*
5. ______ astronomy	E. *insula*
6. ______ aviary	F. *scopulus*
7. ______ terrify	G. *canis*

**Latin origin* means the Latin word from which the derivative comes.

D. VERB CHANTS

Fill in the following verb chants and meanings. Do as much as you can from memory and then look up any you are not sure of:

VIDEŌ CHANT

videō	

IMPERFECT TENSE VERB ENDINGS

-bam	

POSSUM CHANT

possum	

PERFECT TENSE VERB ENDINGS (You don't have to write the meanings!)

-ī	

E. TRANSLATION

Translate the following verbs from the present, imperfect, or future tenses. Underline endings.

1. explōrās ______________________
2. nō ______________________
3. ululābimus ______________________
4. terrēbat ______________________
5. timent ______________________
6. vidēbit ______________________
7. cantābās ______________________
8. volābitis ______________________
9. habēbam ______________________
10. lūcēbunt ______________________
11. flātis ______________________
12. habēbant ______________________

F. CONJUGATIONS

Tell what conjugation (verb family) the following verbs are from. Write *1st* if the verb is from the "A" Family (an *a* before the ending) or *2nd* if the verb is from the "E" Family (an *e* before the ending). Underline the *a* or *e* before each ending. The first one is done as an example.

1. explōrābis ___1st___ 2. terreō ________ 3. cantāmus ________

4. habēbunt ________ 5. flant ________ 6. lūcet ________

G. SAYINGS OF THE WEEK

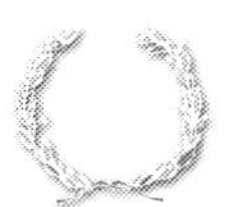

Translate the sayings for this unit:

1. *Montanī semper līberī* ____________________

2. *Cavē canem* ____________________

3. *Piscem natāre docēre* ____________________

4. *Sōl lūcet omnibus* ____________________

5. *In principiō creāvit Deus caelum et terram* ____________________

____

Lesson Twelve - Numbers

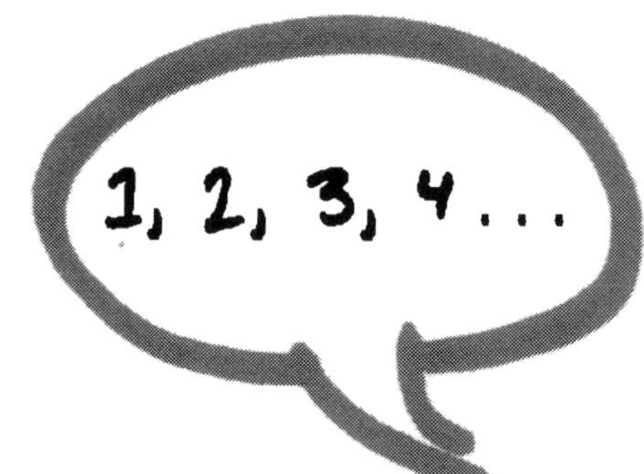

A. VOCABULARY

Memorize the following words and their translations. On a piece of paper, practice writing each word and its translation three times.

Word	Derivative	Translation
1. ūnus	______________________	*one*
2. duo	______________________	*two*
3. trēs	______________________	*three*
4. quattuor	______________________	*four*
5. quinque	______________________	*five*
6. sex	______________________	*six*
7. septem	______________________	*seven*
8. octō	______________________	*eight*
9. novem	______________________	*nine*
10. decem	______________________	*ten*
11. centum	______________________	*a hundred*
12. mille	______________________	*a thousand*
13. numerus	______________________	*number*
14. numerō	______________________	*I count*
15. augeō	______________________	*I increase*

B. VOCABULARY PRACTICE

Write the Latin for the following words:

1. a thousand ______________________
2. nine ______________________
3. two ______________________
4. I increase ______________________
5. four ______________________
6. three ______________________
7. a hundred ______________________
8. ten ______________________
9. eight ______________________
10. one ______________________
11. seven ______________________
12. I count ______________________
13. six ______________________
14. five ______________________
15. number ______________________

C. DERIVATIVES

Answer the following questions by writing the correct number on the blank.

How many years in: a decade? ____________ a century? ____________ a millenium? ____________

How many babies are born when there are: triplets? ______ quadruplets? ______ quintuplets? ______

How many musicians play in a:

duet? ______ trio? ______ quartet? ______ quintet? ______ sextet? ______

How many arms does an octopus have? ______

The word *unicorn* comes from two Latin words, *ūnus* and *cornū* (which means *horn*).

Why is this a good name for the unicorn? ______________________________

Can you list any other derivatives of *ūnus* that start with *uni-*?

*uni-*________________ *uni-* ________________ *uni-* ________________

Sunt duo liberi!

D. NOUN CHANTS

The new chant below is a noun chant. Noun chant endings do not have meanings in the same way that verb endings do. Instead, noun endings can tell what part of speech a word is, such as the subject noun. Like verbs, nouns have different families which are called **declensions.**

Copy and memorize the First Declension Noun Chant below:

FIRST DECLENSION ("A" Family)

Singular	Plural
-a	-ae
-ae	-ārum
-ae	-īs
-am	-ās
-ā	-īs

Look back through old words lists and find ten nouns that are from first declension. You are looking for words that are persons, places, or things which end in *a*, such as *puella*.

1. ____________________
2. ____________________
3. ____________________
4. ____________________
5. ____________________
6. ____________________
7. ____________________
8. ____________________
9. ____________________
10. ____________________

E. TRANSLATION

Translate the verbs *augeō* and *numerō* with endings from the present, imperfect, and future tenses. Underline endings.

1. augētis ______________________
2. numerābant ______________________
3. augēmus ______________________
4. numerābō ______________________
5. augēbat ______________________
6. numerābis ______________________

F. SAYING OF THE WEEK

Ē plūribus ūnum (One out of many)

This is the motto of the United States of America

Write the saying of the week and its meaning below.

Saying: ______________________

Meaning: ______________________

G. REVIEW LIST

1. tempestās *weather, storm*
2. imber *rain*
3. nix *snow*
4. ventus *wind*
5. flō *I blow*
6. astrum *constellation*
7. lībra *pair of scales*
8. geminus *twin*
9. orca *whale*
10. cervus *deer*

Lesson Thirteen - Thanksgiving

Iulia Iulius Est avia. Est avus.

A. VOCABULARY

Memorize the following words and their translations. On a piece of paper, practice writing each word and its translation three times.

Word	Derivative	Translation
1. supplicātio	______________________________	*thanksgiving*
2. grātīae	______________________________	*thanks*
3. nihil est*	______________________________	*you're welcome*
4. cornū	______________________________	*horn*
5. cōpia	______________________________	*plenty, supply*
6. coquus	______________________________	*cook*
7. epulae	______________________________	*feast*
8. sī placet	______________________________	*please*
9. dō	______________________________	*I give*
10. avus	______________________________	*grandfather*
11. avia	______________________________	*grandmother*

**Nihil est* literally means "it's nothing."

B. VOCABULARY PRACTICE

Write the Latin meaning for the following words:

1. thanks ______________________________
2. I give ______________________________
3. feast ______________________________
4. cook ______________________________
5. please ______________________________
6. you're welcome ______________________________
7. horn ______________________________
8. thanksgiving ______________________________
9. plenty, supply ______________________________
10. grandmother ______________________________
11. grandfather ______________________________

C. Derivatives

Cornucopia combines two Latin words. Cornucopias often appear as decorations at Thanksgiving. What is another name for a *cornucopia*?

____

Epulae

Draw a picture of a *cornucopia.*

D. CONJUGATION AND TRANSLATION

Dō is a first conjugation (or "A" Family) verb. Conjugate and translate *dō* in the boxes below. Remember, the *ō* changes to an *a* before the endings.

PRESENT TENSE

dō -	

IMPERFECT TENSE

dābam -	

FUTURE TENSE

dābo -	

E. TRANSLATION

Now translate some review verbs with endings from the present, imperfect, and future tenses. Underline endings.

1. auget ______________________
2. flant ______________________
3. ululābis ______________________
4. lūcēbam ______________________
5. volābitis ______________________
6. vidēbāmus ______________________

F. SAYING OF THE WEEK

Dāte, et dābitur vobīs (Give, and it shall be given to you. Luke 6:38)

Write the saying of the week and its meaning below:

Saying: ______________________

Meaning: ______________________

NO REVIEW WORDS THIS WEEK!

Lesson Fourteen - Time

A. VOCABULARY

Memorize the following words and their translations. On a piece of paper, practice writing each word and its translation three times.

Word	Derivative	Translation
1. tempus	______________	*time*
2. annus	______________	*year*
3. mensis	______________	*month*
4. hōra	______________	*hour*
5. punctum	______________	*minute*
6. sōlārīum	______________	*sundial*
7. merīdiēs	______________	*noon*
8. ante	______________	*before*
9. post	______________	*after*
10. herī	______________	*yesterday*
11. hodiē	______________	*today*
12. crās	______________	*tomorrow*
13. nunc	______________	*now*
14. moveō	______________	*I move*
15. properō	______________	*I hurry*

B. VOCABULARY PRACTICE

Translate the following words into Latin:

1. I move ____________________
2. hour ____________________
3. sundial ____________________
4. minute ____________________
5. today ____________________
6. noon ____________________
7. yesterday ____________________
8. month ____________________
9. before ____________________
10. I hurry ____________________
11. year ____________________
12. tomorrow ____________________
13. after ____________________
14. time ____________________
15. now ____________________

C. DERIVATIVES

Look up the following derivatives in an English dictionary. Write the definition of each derivative and give its Latin origin.

1. punctual ____________________

 Latin origin: ____________________

2. anterior ____________________

 Latin origin: ____________________

3. posterior ____________________

 Latin origin: ____________________

4. annual: ____________________

 Latin origin: ____________________

5. procrastinate: ____________________

 Latin origin: ____________________

D. NOUN CHANTS

Here is a new noun chant to learn. It is called **Second Declension**, or the "US" Family.

SECOND DECLENSION

-us	-ī
-ī	-ōrum
-ō	-īs
-um	-ōs
-ō	-īs

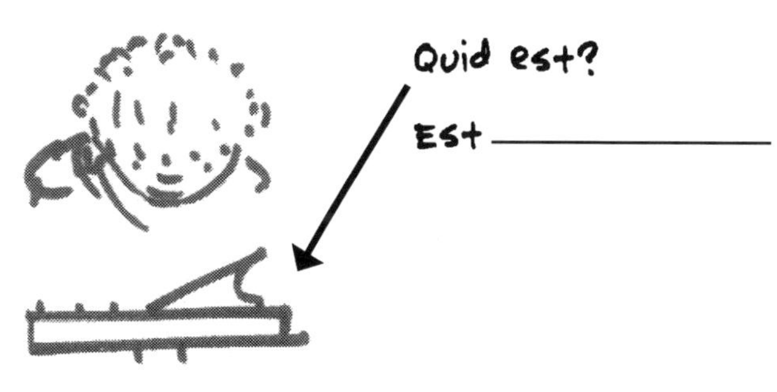

Practice writing the new chant:

Now review the First Declension Noun Chant. Notice the words written to the left of the chant. These are called the *five noun cases*. Noun case endings show what part of speech a Latin noun is.

CASE	Singular	Plural
Nominative	-a	-ae
Genitive	-ae	-ārum
Dative	-ae	-īs
Accusative	-am	-ās
Ablative	-ā	-īs

We will only be using the **nominative case** for now. The nominative endings are the top row and mean that a noun is the *subject* of a sentence.

SN V
For example: *Puella properat*. (The girl hurries.) *Puella* is the subject noun.

Study the second declension noun endings and five noun cases below:

CASE	Singular	Plural
Nominative	-us	-ī
Genitive	-ī	-ōrum
Dative	-ō	-īs
Accusative	-um	-ōs
Ablative	-ō	-īs

Again, the top row contains the *nominative* endings. These endings go on Latin subject nouns in second declension.

SN V
For example: *Lupus movet.* (The wolf moves.) *Lupus* is the subject noun.

Here is an easy way to remember the five noun cases:

Nominative - No
Genitive - Gentle
Dative - Dad
Accusative - Accuses
Ablative - Apples

Practice writing the five noun cases on the lines below:

____

____

____

____

____

Note this well: Latin does NOT use articles like *the* and *a*.

E. TRANSLATION

Translate the following sentences. All are Pattern 1 (subject noun-verb). Label subject nouns with *SN* and verbs with *V*.

1. Puella movet. ______________________________
2. Hōra volābit. ______________________________
3. Gallus properābat. ______________________________
4. Gallīna movēbit. ______________________________

F. SAYING OFF THE WEEK

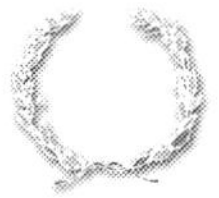

Tempus fugit (Time flies)

Write the saying and the meaning below.

Saying: ______________________________

Meaning: ______________________________

G. REVIEW LIST

1. grātīae — *thanks*
2. sī placet — *please*
3. nihil est — *its nothing*
4. dō — *I give*
5. augeō — *I increase*
6. numerus — *number*
7. mille — *a thousand*
8. calidus — *hot*
9. gelidus — *cold*
10. aquārius — *water carrier*

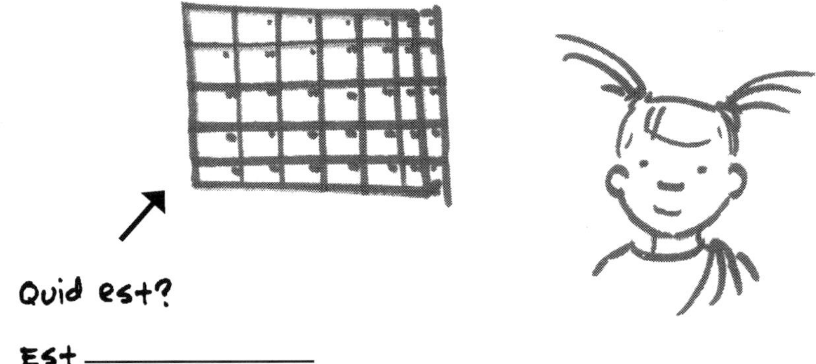

Lesson Fifteen - The Body

A. VOCABULARY

Memorize the following words and their translations. On a piece of paper, practice writing each word and its translation three times.

Word	Derivative	Translation
1. corpus	______________________	*body*
2. caput	______________________	*head*
3. oculus	______________________	*eye*
4. auris	______________________	*ear*
5. nāsus	______________________	*nose*
6. ōs	______________________	*mouth*
7. dens	______________________	*tooth*
8. brācchium	______________________	*arm*
9. manus	______________________	*hand*
10. digitus	______________________	*finger*
11. crūs	______________________	*leg*
12. pēs	______________________	*foot*
13. cor	______________________	*heart*
14. exerceō	______________________	*I train, exercise*
15. spirō	______________________	*I breathe*

B. TRANSLATION

Translate the following words into Latin:

1. I train, exercise ____________________
2. heart ____________________
3. leg ____________________
4. head ____________________
5. arm ____________________
6. tooth ____________________
7. I breathe ____________________
8. nose ____________________
9. ear ____________________
10. foot ____________________
11. hand ____________________
12. finger ____________________
13. body ____________________
14. mouth ____________________
15. eye ____________________

C. DERIVATIVES

Fill in the blanks with derivatives we have discussed in the vocabulary section. Tell which *Latin* word each derivative comes from.

1. When you want your *corpus* to be in good shape, you need to ______________________________ .

    This derivative comes from the Latin word ______________________________

2. When you do something by hand (instead of using a machine) you are doing it ______________ .

    This derivative comes from the Latin word ______________________________

3. When you give a report out loud (instead of writing it), you are giving an ______________ report.

    This derivative comes from the Latin word ______________________________

4. When an *orca* breathes, it uses a ______________________________ .

    This derivative comes from the Latin word ______________________________

D. NOUN CHANTS

Memorize the new noun chant below. It is called **Second Declension Neuter,** and is a cousin of Second Declension. Compare Second Declension Neuter with regular Second Declension. Highlight the places where Second Declension Neuter is different.

Second Declension

-us	-ī
-ī	-ōrum
-ō	-īs
-um	-ōs
-ō	-īs

Second Declension Neuter

-um	-a
-ī	-ōrum
-ō	-īs
-um	-a
-ō	-īs

Using the abbreviation "Nom." for *nominative case*, label the top row of Second Declension Neuter.

See if you can write the noun cases from memory on the lines below. After you are done, check your answers by looking in Lesson 14, Section D. Correct any that are spelled incorrectly.

1. ______________________________

2. ______________________________

3. ______________________________

4. ______________________________

5. ______________________________

E. TRANSLATION

Translate these Pattern 1 sentences. Label the subject noun and verb before you translate.

1. Puer exercet. ______________________________

2. Fēminae exercēbant. ______________________________

3. Orca spirābit. ______________________________

4. Tempus volat. ______________________________

F. SAYING OF THE WEEK

Dum spirō sperō (While I breathe, I hope)

This is the motto of South Carolina.

Write the saying of the week and its meaning below:

Saying: ______________________________

Meaning: ______________________________

G. REVIEW LIST

1. moveō *I move*
2. properō *I hurry*
3. sōlārīum *sundial*
4. ante *before*
5. post *after*
6. epulae *feast*
7. ūnus *one*
8. decem *ten*
9. umbra *shade*
10. vaga *planet*

Lesson Sixteen - Christmas

A. VOCABULARY

Memorize the following words and their translations. On a piece of paper, practice writing each word and its translation three times.

Word	Derivative	Translation
1. Iēsūs	______________________________	*Jesus*
2. Christus	______________________________	*Christ*
3. diēs nātālis	______________________________	*birthday*
4. praesepe	______________________________	*manger*
5. angelus	______________________________	*angel*
6. magus	______________________________	*wise man*
7. infans	______________________________	*baby*
8. ruber	______________________________	*red*
9. viridis	______________________________	*green*
10. asinus	______________________________	*donkey*
11. glōria	______________________________	*glory*

B. VOCABULARY PRACTICE

Translate these words into Latin.

1. red ______________________
2. Jesus ______________________
3. angel ______________________
4. birthday ______________________
5. baby ______________________
6. green ______________________
7. glory ______________________
8. manger ______________________
9. wise man ______________________
10. donkey ______________________
11. Christ ______________________

C. DERIVATIVES

Draw a line from the derivative to its Latin origin:

DERIVATIVE	LATIN ORIGIN
Christian	*ruber*
ass	*angelus*
glorious	*viridis*
magician	*magus*
ruby	*Chrīstus*
viridescent	*asinus*
angelic	*glōria*

D. REVIEW CHANTS

Fill in the following review chants. Give meanings when required.

FIRST CONJUGATION

amō -	

SECOND CONJUGATION

videō -	

LINKING VERB (PRESENT TENSE)

sum –	

POSSUM CHANT

possum –	

PRESENT TENSE VERB ENDINGS

-ō –	

FUTURE TENSE VERB ENDINGS

-bō –	

IMPERFECT TENSE VERB ENDINGS

-bam –	

PERFECT TENSE VERB ENDINGS

-ī –	

FIRST DECLENSION

-a –	

SECOND DECLENSION

-us –	

SECOND DECLENSION NEUTER

-um –	

Quis sunt?

Sunt magi.

E. FILL IN THE BLANKS

Fill in the blanks with the correct Latin words to tell the Christmas story. Choose words from this week's list and the review words for this week. Some words might be used more than once.

Joseph and Mary went to Bethlehem to be counted. Mary rode on an (1)____________________. Because there was no room at the inn in Bethlehem, Mary and Joseph had to sleep in a (2)____________________. When Mary had her (3)____________________, she laid him in a (4) ____________________. They named the baby (5)____________________. An (6)____________________ appeared with the heavenly host to some (7)____________________**(ēs)*** who were taking care of their (8) ____________________**(ēs)***. The (9)____________________ hurried to Bethlehem to see the new born (10)____________________. Later, three (11) ____________________ followed a (12) ____________________ to the stable and brought gifts to the baby (13)____________________. The *māter, pater, angelī, pastorēs, and magī* all gave (14)____________________ to God for the birth of (15)____________________ (16)____________________.

*-*ēs* is the plural ending for these words. We have not studied this ending yet.

F. SAYING OF THE WEEK

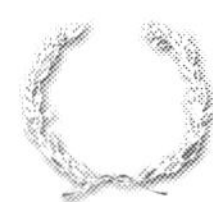 *Glōria in excelsīs Deō* (Glory to God in the highest)

Write the saying of the week and its meaning below:

Saying: ______________________________

Meaning: ______________________________

G. REVIEW LIST

1. stabulum *stable*
2. pastor *shepherd*
3. ovis *sheep*
4. bōs *cow*
5. stella *star*
6. caelum *sky*
7. arbor *tree*
8. māter *mother*
9. pater *father*
10. grātīae *thanks*

Quid est?

Est ______________

Lesson Seventeen - Clothing

A. VOCABULARY

Memorize the following words and their translations. On a piece of paper, practice writing each word and its translation three times.

Word	Derivative	Translation
1. vestis		*clothing, garment*
2. brācae		*pants*
3. tunica		*tunic, shirt*
4. stola		*dress*
5. toga		*toga*
6. palla		*cloak*
7. calceus		*shoe*
8. caliga		*boot*
9. globulus		*button*
10. lāna		*wool*
11. ānulus		*ring*
12. armilla		*bracelet*
13. ornō		*I decorate, equip*
14. lavō		*I wash, bathe*
15. gestō		*I wear*

B. TRANSLATION

Translate these words into Latin:

1. boot ______________________
2. wool ______________________
3. bracelet ______________________
4. I wear ______________________
5. I decorate, equip ______________________
6. tunic, shirt ______________________
7. clothing, garment ______________________
8. pants ______________________
9. dress ______________________
10. cloak ______________________
11. ring ______________________
12. shoe ______________________
13. I wash, bathe ______________________
14. button ______________________
15. toga ______________________

C. DERIVATIVES

Fill in the blanks with derivatives from this week's list . Give the Latin origin.

1. If someone has a weak leg, he might wear a ______________________________ .

   Latin origin: ______________________________

2. A sleeveless garment worn over other clothing is called a ______________________________ .

   Latin origin: ______________________________

3. You decorate a Christmas tree with ______________________________ .

   Latin origin: ______________________________

Challenge Derivative! In what part of the body would you find the *calcaneus* bone? ______________

What Latin word on our list is *calcaneus* related to? ______________________________

D. NOUN CHANTS

Fill in the missing blanks on the noun chants below without looking. Then look at your chant charts to check your work. Correct any spelling errors.

FIRST DECLENSION

-a	
-ae	-ārum
	-īs
-ā	-īs

SECOND DECLENSION

-us	
-ō	-īs
-um	
	-īs

SECOND DECLENSION NEUTER

-um	
	-ōrum
-ō	-īs
-ō	-īs

Now review three ways to translate the present tense.

1. no helping verb
2. *am, is, are*
3. *do, does*

Translate *lavō* in three ways:

1. ____

2. ____

3. ____

E. TRANSLATION

Translate the following sentences. Label before you translate.

1. Māter gestat. ____________________
2. Canis lavābat. ____________________
3. Lavābō. ____________________
4. Gestābimus. ____________________
5. Puer ornābat. ____________________
6. Ornant. ____________________

F. SAYING OF THE WEEK

Ante Christum nātus (Before Christ's birth)

Write the saying and meaning of the week below.

Saying: ____________________

Meaning: ____________________

G. REVIEW LIST

1. infans — *baby*
2. Chrīstus — *Christ*
3. magus — *wise man*
4. oculus — *eye*
5. auris — *ear*
6. nāsus — *nose*
7. brācchium — *arm*
8. spirō — *I breathe*
9. annus — *year*
10. octō — *eight*

Unit Three Review - Lessons 12 through 17

A. VOCABULARY (Latin to English)

Study Lists 12-17 for three to five minutes. Without looking, write down the English meanings for as many of the following words as you can remember. Finally, check your answers by looking back through Lists 12-17. Use a red pen to write in the correct answers of those you missed or left blank.

1. ūnus ______________________
2. centum ______________________
3. grātīae ______________________
4. dō ______________________
5. corpus ______________________
6. spirō ______________________
7. Iēsūs ______________________
8. ruber ______________________
9. tempus ______________________
10. post ______________________
11. lavō ______________________
12. vestis ______________________
13. hōra ______________________
14. numerō ______________________
15. septem ______________________
16. cornū ______________________
17. coquus ______________________
18. digitus ______________________
19. caput ______________________
20. asinus ______________________
21. magus ______________________
22. ante ______________________
23. annus ______________________
24. gestō ______________________
25. armilla ______________________

B. VOCABULARY (English to Latin)

Study Lists 12-17 for three to five minutes. This time look at the English word first and then look at the Latin form. From memory, write as many of the *Latin* words as you can remember. Don't worry too much about spelling. When you are finished, look up the ones you don't remember and write the correct answers using a red pen.

1. four ____________	14. eight ____________
2. a thousand ____________	15. number ____________
3. please ____________	16. thanksgiving ____________
4. you're welcome ____________	17. plenty, supply ____________
5. minute ____________	18. today ____________
6. tomorrow ____________	19. I move ____________
7. heart ____________	20. leg ____________
8. tooth ____________	21. nose ____________
9. green ____________	22. angel ____________
10. glory ____________	23. Christ ____________
11. pants ____________	24. boot ____________
12. dress ____________	25. I decorate, equip ____________
13. shoe, slipper ____________	

C. DERIVATIVES

Write a Derivative for each of the following words:

WORD	DERIVATIVE
1. globulus	____________
2. angelus	____________
3. manus	____________
4. ante	____________
5. post	____________
6. grātīae	____________
7. centum	____________
8. ūnus	____________
9. spirō	____________
10. ornō	____________

D. Review Chants

Fill in the following review chants. Do as much as you can from memory and then look up any you are not sure of.

FIRST DECLENSION

-a	

SECOND DECLENSION

-us	

SECOND DECLENSION NEUTER

-um	

Underline endings on the nouns below. Then write the number of the declension each noun is from. You may abbreviate using *1st, 2nd, or 2nd N.* One is done as an example.

1. cōpia ___*1st*___ 2. brācchium ________ 3. ānulus ________

4. numerus ________ 5. stola ________ 6. toga ________

E. NOUN CASES

Below are the five noun cases. Practice writing the five noun cases on the lines below.

(a trick to remember five noun cases)

Nominative ____________________ NO

Genitive ____________________ GENTLE

Dative ____________________ DAD

Accusative ____________________ ACCUSES

Ablative ____________________ APPLES

Remember, Latin subject nouns always have *nominative case endings*.

F. TRANSLATION

Translate the following Pattern 1 sentences. Label the subject noun and verb.

1. Coquus numerat. ______

2. Digitus movēbat. ______

3. Nāsus spirat. ______

Now translate verbs only. Underline the verb endings.

1. ornābimus ______

2. exercēbunt ______

3. properābās ______

4. gestātis ______

5. dō ______

6. dābō ______

7. dābam ______

G. SAYINGS OF THE WEEK

Translate the sayings for this unit:

1. *Ē plūribus ūnum* ______

   This is the motto for what country? ______

2. *Dāte, et dābitur vobīs* ______

3. *Tempus fugit* ______

4. *Dum spirō spērō* ______________________________

This is the motto for what state? ______________________________

5. *Glōria in excelsīs Deō* ______________________________

6. *Ante Christum nātum* ______________________________

Lesson Eighteen - Ships and Sailing

A. VOCABULARY

Memorize the following words and their translations. On a piece of paper, practice writing each Latin word and its translation three times.

Word	Derivative	Translation
1. nāvis	____________________	*ship*
2. ratis	____________________	*raft*
3. velum	____________________	*sail, curtain*
4. ancora	____________________	*anchor*
5. rēmus	____________________	*oar*
6. mare	____________________	*sea*
7. unda	____________________	*wave (of the sea)*
8. ōra	____________________	*shore*
9. nauta	____________________	*sailor*
10. pīrāta	____________________	*pirate*
11. aurum	____________________	*gold*
12. gemma	____________________	*jewel*
13. nāvigō	____________________	*I sail*
14. gubernō	____________________	*I steer*
15. rēmigo	____________________	*I row*

B. VOCABULARY PRACTICE

Write the Latin for the following words:

1. jewel ______________________
2. raft ______________________
3. I steer ______________________
4. anchor ______________________
5. sea ______________________
6. pirate ______________________
7. shore ______________________
8. I row ______________________
9. I sail ______________________
10. gold ______________________
11. sailor ______________________
12. wave ______________________
13. oar ______________________
14. ship ______________________
15. sail, curtain ______________________

C. DERIVATIVES

Match the following derivatives on the left to their Latin origins on the right by drawing a line from the derivative to the Latin word.

DERIVATIVES	LATIN ORIGINS
aquarium	*mare*
veil	*aqua*
submarine	*gubernō*
navigate	*nāvigō*
nautical	*velum*
govern	*nauta*

D. VERB CHANTS

Memorize the new verb chant below. It is called the **Future Perfect Tense.** You do not need to learn meanings for it.

FUTURE PERFECT TENSE VERB ENDINGS

-erō	-erimus
-eris	-eritis
-erit	-erint

Now practice writing the new chant:

E. PLURAL NOUNS

In English, we make nouns plural by adding *-s* or sometimes *-es*. In Latin, we can also add plural endings, but *which* plural ending we choose depends on the declension (or noun family) that the word is from. For now, we will only make **subject nouns** plural. Remember, subject nouns go in the nominative case.

Study the examples below:

If a noun is in first declension, the singular *a* becomes the plural *ae.*

*puell***a** (girl) becomes *puell***ae** (girls)

If a noun is in second declension, the singular *us* becomes the plural *ī.*

*porc***us** (pig) becomes *porc***ī** (pigs)

In the first and second declension chants below, highlight the nominative plural endings only.

First Declension

CASE	SINGULAR	PLURAL
Nom.	-a	-ae
Gen.	-ae	-ārum
Dat.	-ae	-īs
Acc.	-am	-ās
Abl.	-ā	-īs

Second Declension

CASE	SINGULAR	PLURAL
Nom.	-us	-ī
Gen.	-ī	-ōrum
Dat.	-ō	-īs
Acc.	-um	-ōs
Abl.	-ō	-īs

Make the following nouns plural and tell what each plural noun means. The first two are done for you.

SINGULAR NOUN	PLURAL NOUN	PLURAL TRANSLATION
1. nauta	nautae	sailors
2. rēmus	rēmī	oars
3. pīrāta	______	______
4. globulus	______	______
5. gemma	______	______
6. ānulus	______	______

F. TRANSLATION

Translate the following sentences. Some of them contain plural nouns. When a subject noun is plural the verb must be plural also. Label sentences.

1. Nautae remigant. ______
2. Nauta gubernat. ______
3. Pīrāta nāvigābit. ______

4. Pīrātae properābunt.____

5. Rēmus movēbat.____

6. Rēmī movēbant.____

G. SAYING OF THE WEEK

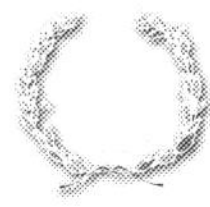

Notā bene (Note well)

Often in books *notā bene* is abbreviated as N.B. When you see N.B. or Notā Bene you should pay special attention to what is written afterwards - it's important!

Write the saying of the week and its meaning on the lines below.

Saying: ____

Meaning: ____

H. REVIEW LIST

1. brācae	*pants*
2. calceus	*shoe*
3. globulus	*button*
4. lāna	wool
5. lavō	*I wash*
6. Iēsūs	*Jesus*
7. manus	*hand*
8. merīdiēs	*noon*
9. coquus	*cook*
10. arcus pluvius	*rainbow*
11. laboro	*I work*

Lesson Nineteen - Wars and Castles

A. VOCABULARY

Memorize the following words and their translations. On a piece of paper, practice writing each Latin word and its translation three times.

Word	Derivative	Translation
1. lēgātus	______________________	*lieutenant*
2. mīles	______________________	*soldier*
3. rēx	______________________	*king*
4. rēgīna	______________________	*queen*
5. castellum	______________________	*castle*
6. mūrus	______________________	*wall*
7. hasta	______________________	*spear*
8. gladius	______________________	*sword*
9. sagitta	______________________	*arrow*
10. bellum	______________________	*war*
11. inimīcus	______________________	*enemy*
12. vulnerō	______________________	*I wound*
13. necō	______________________	*I kill*
14. imperō	______________________	*I order*
15. pugnō	______________________	*I fight*

B. VOCABULARY PRACTICE

Write the Latin for the following words:

1. I order ______________________
2. enemy ______________________
3. lieutenant ______________________
4. sword ______________________
5. I fight ______________________
6. spear ______________________
7. castle ______________________
8. war ______________________
9. king ______________________
10. I wound ______________________
11. queen ______________________
12. arrow ______________________
13. wall ______________________
14. I kill ______________________
15. soldier ______________________

Quid est?

Est ______________

Quid est?

Est ______________

C. DERIVATIVES

Underline the correct answer for each derivative below.

1. If someone is in the *military*, he is a:

   a) factory worker   b) soldier   c) doctor

   What Latin word does *military* come from? ______________________

2. If someone is *pugnacious* he likes to:

   a) fight   b) paint   c) play

   What Latin word does *pugnacious* come from? ______________________

3. An *imperative* sentence:

   a) asks a question   b) shows strong feelings   c) commands

   What Latin word does *imperative* come from? ______________________

D. VERB CHANTS

Memorize the new verb chant below. It is called the **Pluperfect Tense.** You do not need to learn the meanings for it. Look for a verb pattern you have seen before and highlight those endings.

PLUPERFECT TENSE VERB ENDINGS

-eram	-erāmus
-erās	-erātis
-erat	-erant

Quid est?

Est ______________

Practice writing the Pluperfect Tense Chant:

Quis est?

Est ____________

E. PLURAL NOUNS

Make the following Latin nouns plural and then give their plural translations. Look at Lesson 18 E to review making nouns plural.

Singular Noun	Plural Noun	Plural Translation
1. sagitta	____________	____________
2. lēgātus	____________	____________
3. gladius	____________	____________
4. rēgīna	____________	____________
5. mūrus	____________	____________

These nouns are from first ("A" Family) and second ("US" Family) declensions. Now let's make nouns plural in *second declension neuter.* Study the chart below and highlight the nominative plural ending.

Second Declension Neuter

CASE	SINGULAR	PLURAL
Nom.	-um	-a
Gen.	-ī	-ōrum
Dat.	-ō	-īs
Acc.	-um	-a
Abl.	-ō	-īs

To make a second declension neuter noun plural in the nominative case, remove the *-um* ending and add *-a*.

For example:	Singular	Plural
	castellum (castle)	*castella* (castles)

N.B. Be careful when translating second declension neuter plural nouns. They look like another noun ending in a different declension. Can you tell which declension? ____________________

There is one other second declension neuter noun ("UM" Family) on our list. Write it on the line below and make it plural, then give its plural translation.

Singular Noun	Plural Noun	Plural Translation
____________________	____________________	____________________

F. TRANSLATION

Translate the following verbs. Underline endings.

1. vulnerābātis ____________________
2. imperābimus ____________________
3. necābās ____________________
4. pugnābō ____________________

Now practice translating sentences. Underline endings on nouns and verbs. Label SN and V.

1. Inimīcus vulnerat. ____________________
2. Inimīcī vulnerant. ____________________
3. Rēgīna imperābit. ____________________
4. Rēgīnae imperābunt. ____________________
5. Lēgātus pugnābat. ____________________
6. Lēgātī pugnābant. ____________________

G. Saying of the Week

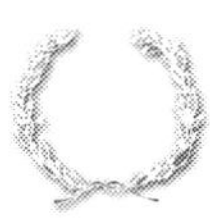

Pax potior bellō (Peace is more powerful than war)

Write the saying of the week and its meaning on the lines below.

Saying: ______________________________

Meaning: ______________________________

H. Review List

1. nāvis — *ship*
2. mare — *sea*
3. ōra — *shore*
4. nauta — *sailor*
5. gubernō — *I steer*
6. ānulus — *ring*
7. tunica — *tunic*
8. exerceō — *I train*
9. nunc — *now*
10. centum — *a hundred*

Quis est?

Est ______________

Lesson Twenty - Gardens

A. VOCABULARY

Memorize the following words and their translations. On a piece of paper, practice writing each Latin word and its translation three times.

Word	Derivative	Translation
1. hortus	__________	*garden*
2. herba	__________	*plant*
3. flōs	__________	*flower*
4. folium	__________	*leaf*
5. grāmen	__________	*grass*
6. mālum	__________	*apple*
7. pōmārium	__________	*orchard*
8. ūva	__________	*grape*
9. vīnea	__________	*vineyard*
10. bestiola	__________	*insect*
11. apis	__________	*bee*
12. pāla	__________	*shovel*
13. fōns	__________	*fountain*
14. fodicō	__________	*I dig*
15. floreō	__________	*I bloom, flourish*

B. VOCABULARY PRACTICE

Write the Latin meaning for the following words:

1. leaf ______________________________
2. insect ______________________________
3. I bloom, flourish ______________________________
4. fountain ______________________________
5. shovel ______________________________
6. plant ______________________________
7. orchard ______________________________
8. vineyard ______________________________
9. grape ______________________________
10. grass ______________________________
11. I dig ______________________________
12. apple ______________________________
13. bee ______________________________
14. garden ______________________________
15. flower ______________________________

C. DERIVATIVES

Look up the following words in an English dictionary. Tell what Latin word each one comes from.

1. horticulture: ______________________________

____

Latin origin: ______________________________

2. floriculture: ______________________________

____

Latin origin: ______________________________

3. viticulture: ______________________________

____

Latin origin: ______________________________

N.B. The English word *culture* comes from a Latin word, *colō*, which means to till or tend the soil.

D. ACCUSATIVE CASE (DIRECT OBJEECTS)

Review the five noun cases below:

Nominative - used for subject nouns
Genitive
Dative
Accusative -used for direct objects
Ablative

Quid est?

Est ______________

So far, we have only used the nominative case endings when we want to have a subject noun in a sentence. Also, we have only translated Pattern 1 sentences containing a subject noun and a verb. Now we will introduce Pattern 2 sentences which also contain a **direct object.** Look at the Pattern 1 sentence below:

SN V
Puer fodicat. *The boy digs.*

A direct object answers the question *what? What* does the boy dig? The Pattern 2 sentence below answers the question *what.*

SN DO V-t
Puer herbam fodicat. *The boy digs a plant.*

Notice that the direct object (abbreviated *DO*) usually goes in front of the verb in Latin sentences. Also notice the underlined ending on the direct object *herbam*. The ending on this word is in the accusative case. Just as subject nouns are always *nominative,* direct objects are always *accusative.*

N.B. In Pattern 2 sentences, label the verb *V-t* which stands for **verb transitive.**

Here is another example of a sentence containing a direct object:

SN DO V-t
Agricola hortum arat. *The farmer plows the garden.*

Now study the *plural* examples below.

SN DO V- t
Puerī herbās fodicant. *The boys dig the plants.*

SN DO V-t
Agricolae hortōs arant. *The farmers plow the gardens.*

Highlight or underline the accusative endings in the following noun chants.

N.B. In second declension neuter, the nominative and accusative endings look the same.

FIRST DECLENSION

Case	Sing.	Pl.
Nom.	-a	-ae
Gen.	-ae	-ārum
Dat.	-ae	-īs
Acc.	-am	-ās
Abl.	ā	īs

SECOND DECLENSION

Case	Sing.	Pl.
Nom.	-us	-ī
Gen.	-ī	-ōrum
Dat.	-ō	-īs
Acc.	-um	-ōs
Abl.	-ō	-īs

SECOND DECLENSION NEUTER

Case	Sing.	Pl.
Nom.	-um	-a
Gen.	-ī	-ōrum
Dat.	-ō	-īs
Acc.	-um	-a
Abl.	-ō	-īs

Quid est?

Est ______________

E. ACCUSATIVE CASE PRACTICE

Underline the endings on all words in the Pattern 2 sentences below. Label SN, DO, and V-t. Remember that *V-t* stands for "verb transitive" and is used for verbs which are used with direct objects. After labeling, translate sentences.

1. Puella bestiolam necat. ____________________

2. Puer saxum movēbit ____________________

3. Magistra discipulōs numerābat. ____________________

4. Ursus spēluncam explōrat. ____________________

5. Lēgātī inimīcōs pugnant. ____________________

F. SAYING OF THE WEEK

Fructū nōn foliīs arborem aestimā (Judge a tree by its fruit, not by its leaves)

Write the saying of the week and its meaning on the lines below.

Saying: ____________________

Meaning: ____________________

G. REVIEW WORDS

1. lēgātus *lieutenant*
2. pugnō *I fight*
3. inimīcus *enemy*
4. magistra *female teacher*
5. numerō *I count*
6. discipulus *student*
7. explōrō *I explore*
8. necō *I kill*
9. ursus *bear*
10. spēlunca *cave*

Quid est?

Est __________

Lesson Twenty-One - Food

A. VOCABULARY

Memorize the following words and their translations. On a piece of paper, practice writing each word and its translation three times.

Word	Derivative	Translation
1. cibus	__________	*food*
2. ientāculum	__________	*breakfast*
3. prandium	__________	*lunch*
4. cēna	__________	*dinner*
5. pānis	__________	*bread*
6. cāseus	__________	*cheese*
7. būbula	__________	*beef*
8. tomata	__________	*tomato*
9. carōta	__________	*carrot*
10. crustulum	__________	*cookie (little cake)*
11. sūcus	__________	*juice*
12. vīnum	__________	*wine*
13. lībō	__________	*I sip, taste*
14. parō	__________	*I prepare*
15. secō	__________	*I cut*

B. VOCABULARY PRACTICE

Write the Latin for the following words.

1. I sip or taste ____________________
2. I cut ____________________
3. food ____________________
4. cheese ____________________
5. carrot ____________________
6. tomato ____________________
7. juice ____________________
8. beef ____________________
9. wine ____________________
10. I prepare ____________________
11. cookie ____________________
12. bread ____________________
13. dinner ____________________
14. lunch ____________________
15. breakfast ____________________

Quid est?

Est ____________

C. DERIVATIVES

Fill in the blanks below.

1. What derivatives from this list could be ingredients in a salad?

    ____________________ and ____________________

    Latin origin: ____________________ Latin origin: ____________________

2. What derivative can contain a dessert filling? ________________________________

    Latin origin: ____________________

3. What derivative is made from *ūvae* (a word from last week's list)? ____________________

    Latin origin: ____________________

4. This derivative is formed from two Latin words from this week's list, *cum* (which means *with*) and *pānis* (which means *bread*). What is it? ________________________________

D. VERB CHANTS

Memorize the chant below. It is called the **Present Passive.**

PRESENT PASSIVE

-r	-mur
-ris	-minī
-tur	-ntur

Practice writing the new chant.

E. TRANSLATION

Practice translating these Pattern 2 sentences containing subject nouns, verbs and direct objects. Underline the endings and label the parts of speech.

1. Iūlia aquam lībat. ______

2. Iūlius vīnum lībābit. ______

3. Coquus lavat carōtās. ______

4. Būbulam Iūlia secat. ______

5. Coquī ientāculum parābunt. ______

Challenge Sentence! *Lībō sūcum.* ______

(Hint: The subject noun is hiding in the verb ending.)

F. SAYING OF THE WEEK

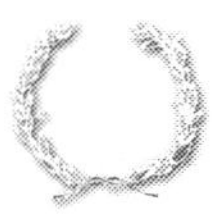

P*ānem et circensēs* (Bread and circuses)

Juvenal, a famous Roman writer, thought the common people in Rome cared only for food and entertainment.

Write the saying of the week and its translation below:

Saying: ______

Meaning: ______

G. REVIEW LIST

1. aqua	*water*	6. hortus	*garden*
2. mālum	*apple*	7. flōs	*flower*
3. ōvum	*egg*	8. ūva	*grape*
4. coquus	*cook*	9. folium	*leaf*
5. culīna	*kitchen*	10. fōns	*fountain*

Lesson Twenty-two - The Arts

A. VOCABULARY

Memorize the following words and their translations. On a piece of paper, practice writing each word and its translation three times.

Word	Derivative	Translation
1. pictūra	____________	*painting, picture*
2. pictor	____________	*painter*
3. pēnicullus	____________	*paintbrush*
4. pigmentum	____________	*paint*
5. fūco	____________	*I color, paint*
6. caeruleus	____________	*blue*
7. flāvus	____________	*yellow*
8. mūsica	____________	*music*
9. mūsicus	____________	*musician*
10. cantus	____________	*song, piece of music*
11. auscultō	____________	*I listen to*
12. fābula	____________	*story*
13. carmen	____________	*poem, song*
14. poēta	____________	*poet*
15. recitō	____________	*I recite, read aloud*

B. VOCABULARY PRACTICE

Write the Latin for the following words:

1. I recite, read aloud ______________________________
2. painting, picture ______________________________
3. poet ______________________________
4. painter ______________________________
5. poem, song ______________________________
6. paintbrush ______________________________
7. story ______________________________
8. paint ______________________________
9. I listen to ______________________________
10. I color, paint ______________________________
11. song, piece of music ______________________________
12. blue ______________________________
13. musician ______________________________
14. yellow ______________________________
15. music ______________________________

C. DERIVATIVES

Look up these derivatives in an English dictionary and write a simple definition on the lines provided. Tell the Latin origin of each derivative.

1. cerulean ____

____

Latin origin? ____

2. pigment ____

____

Latin origin? ____

3. fable ____

____

Latin origin? ____

D. VERB CHANTS

Memorize the new chant below. It is called the **Future Passive.** Do you recognize a pattern that you have seen before? If so, highlight those endings.

FUTURE PASSIVE VERB ENDINGS

-bor	-bimur
-beris	-biminī
-bitur	-buntur

Now practice writing the new chant.

E. PLURAL NOUNS REVIEW

Using your charts, translate these *plural nouns* into Latin. Use the nominative (subject noun) case. The first one is done for you.

1. musicians ______mūsicī______
2. stories ____________________
3. paints ____________________

Now make the same nouns plural in the accusative (direct object) case. Again, the first one is done as an example.

1. musicians ______mūsic**ōs**______
2. stories ____________________
3. paints ____________________

F. TRANSLATION

Translate the following Pattern 1 and Pattern 2 sentences. Underline endings and label parts of speech first! Be sure to look closely at all endings.

1. Poēta fābulam recitat. ____

2. Poētae fābulās recitābunt. ______________________________

____

3. Pictor fucābat pictūram. ______________________________

4. Pictor pēnicullum habet. ______________________________

5. Iūlius mūsicam auscultat. ______________________________

6. Iūlia mūsicum auscultat. ______________________________

G. COLORS

Using markers, crayons, or colored pencils, put the correct color by each word below:

caeruleus ☐ flāvus ☐ ruber ☐ viridis ☐

H. SAYING OF THE WEEK

Poēta nasquitur, nōn fit (A poet is born, not made)

Write the saying of the week and its meaning on the lines below:

Saying: ______________________________

Meaning: ______________________________

Iulius picturam fucat.

Iulius saxum fucat!

I. REVIEW WORDS

1. cantō *I sing*
2. spectō *I look at*
3. habeō *I have*
4. ruber *red*
5. viridis *green*
6. liber *book*
7. flōs *flower*
8. ōs *mouth*
9. hodiē *today*
10. aquila *eagle*

Unit Four Review - Lessons 18 through 22

A. VOCABULARY (Latin to English)

Study Lists 18-22 for three minutes. Without looking, write down the English meanings for as many of the following words as you can remember. Finally, check your answers by looking back through lists 18-22. Use a red pen to write in the correct answers for those you missed or left blank.

1. gubernō ______________________
2. mare ______________________
3. pīrāta ______________________
4. mūrus ______________________
5. vulnerō ______________________
6. hortus ______________________
7. bestiola ______________________
8. ūva ______________________
9. vīnum ______________________
10. cibus ______________________
11. pictor ______________________
12. fābula ______________________
13. caeruleus ______________________
14. nāvigō ______________________
15. nāvis ______________________
16. rēgīna ______________________
17. gladius ______________________
18. bellum ______________________
19. folium ______________________
20. floreō ______________________
21. prandium ______________________
22. secō ______________________
23. sūcus ______________________
24. mūsicus ______________________
25. recitō ______________________

B. VOCABULARY (English to Latin)

Study Lists 18-22 again for three minutes. This time look at the English words first and then look at the Latin form. From memory, write as many of the *Latin* words as you can remember. When you are finished, look up the ones you don't remember and write the correct answers using a red pen.

1. music ____________________
2. poet ____________________
3. paintbrush ____________________
4. I sip, taste ____________________
5. cookie ____________________
6. plant ____________________
7. flower ____________________
8. grass ____________________
9. soldier ____________________
10. I order ____________________
11. wave ____________________
12. sailor ____________________
13. gold ____________________
14. I color, paint ____________________
15. song, piece of music ____________________
16. tomato ____________________
17. I prepare ____________________
18. bread ____________________
19. apple ____________________
20. I dig ____________________
21. king ____________________
22. enemy ____________________
23. castle ____________________
24. jewel ____________________
25. shore ____________________

C. DERIVATIVES

Give the Latin origins for the following derivatives:

1. undulate ____________________
2. military ____________________
3. navigate ____________________
4. imperative ____________________
5. horticulture ____________________
6. crust ____________________

7. companion ______________________ 8. pigment ______________________

9. submarine ______________________ 10. govern ______________________

D. REVIEW CHANTS

Fill in the following chants:

FUTURE PERFECT TENSE VERB ENDINGS

-erō	

PLUPERFECT VERB TENSE ENDINGS

-eram	

PRESENT PASSIVE TENSE ENDINGS

-r	

FUTURE PASSIVE TENSE ENDINGS

-bor	

FIRST DECLENSION

-a	

SECOND DECLENSION

-us	

SECOND DECLENSION NEUTER

-um	

E. PLURAL NOUNS

Make the following nouns plural in the nominative case:

1. carōta ______________________________

2. mālum ______________________________

3. rēmus ______________________________

Now make these same nouns plural in the accusative case:

1. carōta ______________________________

2. mālum ______________________________

3. rēmus ______________________________

F. NOUN CASES

Write out the five noun cases.

____

____

____

____

____

Subject nouns go in the ______________________ case.

Direct objects go in the ______________________ case.

G. TRANSLATION

Translate the following Pattern 2 sentences. Label parts of speech and <u>underline</u> endings.

1. Nauta rēmum movet. ______________________________

2. Inimīcī lēgātōs pugnābant. ______________________________

3. Iūlia hortum parābit. ______________________________

4. Iūlius herbās fodicat. ______________________________

5. Mūsicī poētam auscultant. ______________________________

H. SAYINGS OF THE WEEK

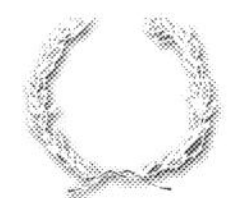

Translate these sayings:

1. *Poēta nasquitur, nōn fit* ______________________________

2. *Pānem et circensēs* ______________________________

3. *Pax potior bellō* ______________________________

4. *Fructū nōn foliīs arborem aestimā* ______________________________

____

5. *Notā bene* ______________________________

Lesson Twenty-three - Geography

A. VOCABULARY

Memorize the following words and their translations. On a piece of paper, practice writing each word and its translation three times.

Word	Derivative	Translation
1. Ītalia	__________	*Italy*
2. Hispānia	__________	*Spain*
3. Germānia	__________	*Germany*
4. Britānnia	__________	*Britain*
5. Gallia	__________	*Gaul*
6. iter	__________	*journey*
7. tabula*	__________	*map*
8. locus	__________	*place*
9. plaustrum	__________	*wagon*
10. carrūca	__________	*carriage*
11. errō	__________	*I wander, I am mistaken*
12. equito	__________	*I ride on horseback*
13. ad	__________	*to, toward*
14. in	__________	*into*
15. patria	__________	*native land*

*On List 4 the word *tabula* meant "board" or "tablet". This word has several other meanings.

B. VOCABULARY PRACTICE

Write the Latin for the following words:

1. native land ________________________
2. I ride on horseback ________________________
3. Spain ________________________
4. into ________________________
5. Germany ________________________
6. Gaul ________________________
7. map ________________________
8. to ________________________
9. place ________________________
10. journey ________________________
11. I wander, I am mistaken ________________________
12. carriage ________________________
13. Britain ________________________
14. wagon ________________________
15. Italy ________________________

C. DERIVATIVES

Identify the mystery derivatives by using the clues below and the Latin origin.

1. My Latin origin is *errō*. When a student says that 2 + 2 = 5, he has committed an

   ____

2. My Latin origin is *locus*. When you find a place on a map, you have found a

   ____

3. My Latin origin is *iter*. When you make a schedule of places you will visit on a trip, you have made an

   ____

D. VERB CHANTS

Memorize the new chant below. It is called the *Imperfect Passive*. Highlight a pattern you have seen before.

IMPERFECT PASSIVE VERB ENDINGS

-bar	-bāmur
-bāris	-bāminī
-bātur	-bantur

Now practice writing the new chant:

E. PREPOSITIONS - "AD" & "IN"

The prepositions *ad* and *in* are used when someone physically moves from one place to another. Study the example below:

	SN	V-t	P		OP
The	*boy*	*walks*	*to*	*the*	*place.*

The word *place* is used as an ***object of the preposition.***

In Latin, the object of the preposition must go in the accusative case, just like direct objects. Now look at the same sentence in Latin.

SN	V-t	P	OP
Puer	*ambulat*	*ad*	*locum.*

Now study this sentence containing the preposition *into.*

	SN	V-t	P	OP
The	*girl*	*wanders*	*into*	*Italy.*

Here is the same example in Latin:

SN	V-t	P	OP
Puella	*errat*	*in*	*Ītaliam.*

Practice translating these sentences containing prepositional phrases. Label parts of speech and underline endings. You do not need to underline endings on prepositions.

1. Fēminae movēbunt in Germāniam. ______________________________

____

2. Iūlius ambulābat ad oppidum. ______________________________

____

3. Vir equitābit in Galliam. ______________________________

____

F. TRANSLATION

Translate the following sentences. Underline endings on words and label parts of speech before you translate.

1. Iūlia tabulam spectat. ______________________

2. Rēx amat patriam. ______________________

3. Nauta ancoram movēbit in aquam. ______________________

G. SAYING OF THE WEEK

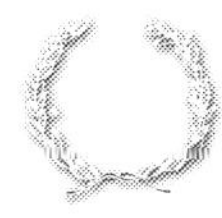

Errāre hūmānum est (to err is human)

Write the saying of the week and its translation below.

Saying: ______________________

Meaning: ______________________

H. REVIEW LIST

1. urbs	*city*
2. oppidum	*town*
3. Rōma	*Rome*
4. vir	*man*
5. fēmina	*woman*
6. puella	*girl*
7. puer	*boy*
8. ambulō	*I walk*
9. habitō	*I live in*
10. sedeō	*I sit*

Lesson Twenty-four - Health

A. VOCABULARY

Memorize the following words and their translations. On a piece of paper, practice writing each Latin word and its translation three times.

Word	Derivative	Translation
1. medicus	______________________	*doctor*
2. medicāmentum	______________________	*medicine*
3. pilūla	______________________	*pill*
4. venēnum	______________________	*poison*
5. somnus	______________________	*sleep*
6. baculum	______________________	*crutch*
7. scientia	______________________	*knowledge*
8. aeger	______________________	*sick*
9. infirmus	______________________	*weak*
10. cūrō	______________________	*I care for*
11. iuvō	______________________	*I help*
12. valeō	______________________	*I am well, strong*
13. dēvorō	______________________	*I swallow*
14. cubō	______________________	*I lie down*
15. nōn	______________________	*not*

B. VOCABULARY PRACTICE

Write the Latin for the following words:

1. I lie down ______________________________
2. I am well, strong ______________________________
3. I care for ______________________________
4. sick ______________________________
5. crutch ______________________________
6. poison ______________________________
7. medicine ______________________________
8. doctor ______________________________
9. pill ______________________________
10. sleep ______________________________
11. knowledge ______________________________
12. weak ______________________________
13. I help ______________________________
14. I swallow ______________________________
15. not ______________________________

C. DERIVATIVES

Choose one derivative from this week's list and look it up in an English dictionary. Write the meaning and Latin origin of the derivative on the lines below and then use the word in an English sentence. One example is done for you.

Derivative: medication

Latin origin: *medicāmentum*

Meaning: a substance for healing or relieving pain

Sentence: The doctor gave Julius a medication for his fever.

Now do your own derivative.

Derivative: ______________________________

Origin: ______________________________

Meaning: ______________________________

Sentence: ______________________________

____

D. NOUN CHANTS

Memorize the chant below. It is called the **Demonstrative Pronoun**. We will only learn the first half of the chant this week. In one way or another, each part of the chant means *this*. Be sure to memorize across, not down like usual.

DEMONSTRATIVE PRONOUN CHANT

hic →	haec →	hoc →
huius →	huius →	huius →
huic →	huic →	huic →
hunc →	hanc →	hoc →
hōc →	hāc →	hōc →

Now practice writing the new chant:

E. THE NEGATIVE "NON" & ADJECTIVES

When we want to make a sentence negative in English we use the adverb *not.* In Latin, the adverb *nōn* is used to make a sentence negative. Compare the examples below.

SN V
Iūlia valet. *Julia is well.*

SN Adv V
Iūlia **nōn** valet. *Julia is not well.*

SN DO V-t
Medicus Iūliam cūrābat. *The doctor was caring for Julia.*

SN DO Adv V-t
Medicus Iūliam **nōn** cūrābat. *The doctor was not caring for Julia.*

In a negative sentence, the adverb *nōn* must go in front of the verb.

N.B. When you translate a negative sentence into English you must use a helping verb. If the verb is from the present tense, choose from *am, is, are, do, does.* If the verb is from the imperfect tense, choose from *was* or *were.* If the verb is from the future tense, choose the helping verb *will.*

ADJECTIVES

You already know that an adjective describes a noun or a pronoun. In this lesson we have two adjectives, *aeger* and *infirmus*. The *-er* on *aeger* is actually in the "US" Family. Both of these adjectives can describe men, boys, or nouns from the second declension ("US" Family).

puer aeger - *the sick boy* 　　　　discipulus infirmus - *the weak boy student*

When we use an adjective to describe women, girls, or nouns from the first declension ("A" Family), we must drop the *-er* or *-us* endings and add an *-a*.

puella aegra - *the sick girl* 　　　　discipula infirma - *the weak girl student*

N.B. In Latin, adjectives often go **after** the noun they describe!

F. TRANSLATION

Now practice what you have learned about adjectives and the adverb *nōn* to translate the sentences below. Be sure to underline endings on all words and label parts of speech (SN, V-t, DO, Adj, P, C, Adv).

1. Medicus bonus puerum iuvat. ______________________________

____

2. Māter fīlium et fīliam cūrābat. ______________________________

____

3. Puer aeger nōn cubābit. ______________________________

____

4. Puella infirma nōn valēbit. ______________________________

____

5. Fīlius aeger venēnum dēvorābat. ______________________________

____

6. Medicus nōn ambulat in domum. ______________________________

____

G. SAYING OF THE WEEK

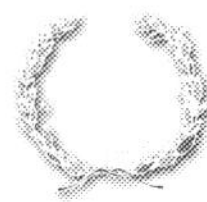 *Medice, cūra tē ipsum* (Physician, heal thyself. Luke 4:23)

Write the saying of the week and its translation on the lines below.

Saying: ____

Meaning: ____

Jesus said these words in his hometown of Nazareth where the people wanted him to perform miracles as he had done in other places. He rebukes them for their lack of faith.

H. REVIEW WORDS

1. lectus — *bed*
2. māter — *mother*
3. fīlius — *son*
4. fīlia — *daughter*
5. domus — *house, home*
6. dō — *I give*
7. ambulō — *I walk*
8. in — *into*
9. ad — *to, toward*
10. bonus — *good*

Lesson Twenty-five - The Church

A. VOCABULARY

Memorize the following words and their translations. On a piece of paper, practice writing each Latin word and its translation three times.

Word	Derivative	Translation
1. Deus	______________________	*God*
2. Biblia Sacra	______________________	*Holy Bible*
3. dominus	______________________	*lord, master*
4. ecclēsia	______________________	*church*
5. ēvangelium	______________________	*good news*
6. apostolus	______________________	*apostle*
7. culpa	______________________	*fault, blame, sin*
8. mors	______________________	*death*
9. sepulchrum	______________________	*tomb*
10. vīta	______________________	*life*
11. vēritās	______________________	*truth*
12. mundus	______________________	*world*
13. narrō	______________________	*I tell*
14. crux	______________________	*cross*
15. servō	______________________	*I save*

B. VOCABULARY PRACTICE

Write the Latin for the following words:

1. cross ______________________
2. death ______________________
3. God ______________________
4. truth ______________________
5. good news ______________________
6. I save ______________________
7. lord, master ______________________
8. world ______________________
9. I tell ______________________
10. Holy Bible ______________________
11. life ______________________
12. fault, blame, sin ______________________
13. apostle ______________________
14. church ______________________
15. tomb ______________________

C. DERIVATIVES

Underline derivatives in the paragraph below that are from List 25 and the review words for this lesson.

God created the world, but man was culpable for sin against God. God sent his son, Jesus, to be our Savior. Jesus took the form of a servant when he died on the cross and was laid in a sepulcher. He rose again and now has dominion over death. His apostles were evangelists who proclaimed this good news. Some apostles were used by God to write parts of the Bible.

D. PRONOUN CHANTS

Review the first half of the demonstrative pronoun chant from Lesson 23 and memorize the second half.

DEMONSTRATIVE PRONOUN CHANT

Review (this)

hic →	haec →	hoc →
huius →	huius →	huius →
huic →	huic →	huic →
hunc →	hanc →	hoc →
hōc →	hāc →	hōc →

New this week! (these)

hī →	hae →	haec →
hōrum →	hārum →	hōrum →
hīs →	hīs →	hīs →
hōs →	hās →	haec →
hīs →	hīs →	hīs →

Now practice writing the **new** half of the chant:

hī		

E. CHANT REVIEWS

For review, fill in the *Sum* Chant and meanings:

sum - *I am*	

F. TRANSLATION

Quis est Iēsūs? (Who is Jesus?). In the Bible, we learn who Jesus is. Often, Jesus himself tells us who he is. Translate the sentences below that tell who Jesus is. Words are from old lists as well as List 24.

1. Iēsūs est dominus. ____________________
2. Iēsūs est vīta. ____________________
3. Iēsūs est vēritās. ____________________
4. Iēsūs est via. ____________________
5. Iēsūs est Chrīstus. ____________________
6. Iēsūs est Deus. ____________________
7. Iēsūs est pānis. ____________________
8. Iēsūs est pastor. ____________________
9. Iēsūs est rēx. ____________________
10. Iēsūs est Fīlius. ____________________

Translate the sentences below. Label parts of speech and underline endings.

1. Apostolī ēvangelium narrābant.

2. Chrīstus mundum servat.

3. Pater Fīlium dat.

G. SAYING OF THE WEEK

Ego sum via, et vēritās, et vīta (I am the Way, the Truth, and the Life. John 14:6)

saying of the week and its meaning below:

Saying:

Meaning:

H. REVIEW WORDS

1. dō *I give*
2. Iēsūs *Jesus*
3. Chrīstus *Christ*
4. via *way*
5. fīlius *son*
6. pater *father*
7. angelus *angel*
8. rēx *king*
9. pānis *bread*
10. vīnum *wine*

Iulius Bibliam Sacram recitat.

Lesson Twenty-six - Entertainment

A. VOCABULARY

Memorize the following words and their translations.
On a piece of paper, practice writing each Latin word and its translation three times.

Word	Derivative	Translation
1. lūdibrium	____________________	*toy*
2. crepundia	____________________	*rattle, toy*
3. pila	____________________	*ball*
4. pūpa	____________________	*doll, puppet*
5. iocus	____________________	*a joke*
6. tabula lūsōriae	____________________	*a game board*
7. theātrum	____________________	*theater*
8. mīma	____________________	*actress*
9. cōmoedus	____________________	*comedian*
10. rīdiculus	____________________	*funny* (as in a situation)
11. simulō	____________________	*I pretend*
12. saltō	____________________	*I dance*
13. rīdeō	____________________	*I laugh, smile*
14. calcitrō	____________________	*I kick*
15. iactō	____________________	*I throw*

N.B. When speaking of a *funny person*, the adjective *iocōsus* is used not *ridiculus*. *Iocōsus* is related to what word in the list above?

B. VOCABULARY PRACTICE

Iulia est iocosa!

Write the Latin for the following words:

1. rattle, toy ______________________
2. ball ______________________
3. joke ______________________
4. theater ______________________
5. comedian ______________________
6. I pretend ______________________
7. I laugh, smile ______________________
8. I throw ______________________
9. toy ______________________
10. doll, puppet ______________________
11. game board ______________________
12. actress ______________________
13. funny (as in a situation) ______________________
14. I dance ______________________
15. I kick ______________________

Bonus Word! Funny (as a person) ______________________

C. DERIVATIVES

Fill in the blanks with English derivatives from List 26.

Julius and Julia love to go to the ______________________ to watch plays.

Julius laughs at the ______________________ who tells funny ______________________ .

Julia likes the beautiful actress. At home, Julia ______________________ the beautiful actress. Julius practices telling silly ________________ that Julia thinks are ______________

Then both children make their own play by moving the strings of their ______________________.

D. PRONOUN CHANTS

There is no new chant this week. Instead, fill in the missing parts of the Demonstrative Pronoun Chant "hic". Remember that this chant means *this* in the singular and *these* in the plural.

DEMONSTRATIVE PRONOUN CHANT

Singular - this

hic		
	huius	
		huic
hunc		
	hāc	

Plural - these

		haec
hōrum		
	hīs	
		haec
hīs		

E. SENTENCE TRANSLATION

Translate the sentences below. Underline endings on nouns and verbs and label parts of speech. Notice whether nouns and verbs are singular or plural. Watch for some prepositional phases.

1. Puer iocōs narrābit. ______________________________

2. Soror rīdet. ______________________________

3. Puellae saltābant ad ludum. ______________________________

____

4. Iūlia pūpam spectat. ______________________________

5. Frāter pilam iactābat in aquam. ______________________________

____

6. Infans crepundia habet. ______________________________

____

N.B. *Crepundia* is the second declension neuter accusative form. This word is plural in Latin but singular in English.

F. MORE SENTENCE TRANSLATION

Translate these sentences. You do not have to label these.

1. Iūlius est cōmoedus. ____________________

____

2. Iūlia nōn est iocōsa. ____________________

____

G. SAYING OF THE WEEK

Rīdē sī sapis (Laugh, if you are wise)

Write the saying of the week and its meaning on the lines below.

Saying: ____________________

Meaning: ____________________

H. Review List

1. lūdus — *school, game*
2. infans — *baby*
3. gladius — *sword*
4. taberna — *shop*
5. inimīcus — *enemy*
6. līberī — *children*
7. spectō — *I watch, look at*
8. narrō — *I tell*
9. pugnō — *I fight*
10. nō — *I swim*

Lesson Twenty-seven - Wedding Celebration

A. VOCABULARY

Memorize the following words and their translations. On a piece of paper, practice writing each Latin word and its translation three times.

Word	Derivative	Translation
1. mātrimōnium	____________________	*marriage*
2. convīvium	____________________	*party, feast*
3. nupta	____________________	*bride*
4. marītus	____________________	*bridegroom*
5. coniunx	____________________	*husband or wife*
6. hospes	____________________	*host, male guest*
7. hospita	____________________	*hostess, female guest*
8. flammeum	____________________	*bridal veil*
9. corōna	____________________	*crown, wreath*
10. rōsa	____________________	*rose*
11. placenta	____________________	*cake*
12. dōnum	____________________	*gift*
13. celebrō	____________________	*I celebrate*
14. gaudeō	____________________	*I rejoice*
15. invītō	____________________	*I invite*

B. VOCABULARY PRACTICE

Write the Latin for the following words:

1. I invite ______________________
2. marriage ______________________
3. I rejoice ______________________
4. party, feast ______________________
5. I celebrate ______________________
6. bride ______________________
7. gift ______________________
8. bridegroom ______________________
9. cake ______________________
10. husband or wife ______________________
11. rose ______________________
12. host, male guest ______________________
13. crown, wreath ______________________
14. hostess, female guest ______________________
15. bridal veil ______________________

C. DERIVATIVES

Match each of the following derivatives to the correct meaning by writing the number of the meaning on the blank. The Latin origins of the derivatives are given in parentheses and will help you match each derivative and its meaning.

DERIVATIVES	MEANINGS
________ convivial (*convīvium*)	1. friendly and kind toward guests
________ conjunction (*coniunx*)	2. fond of feasting, sociable
________ nuptials (*nupta*)	3. a small crown
________ hospitable (*hospes, hospita*)	4. wedding ceremony
________ coronet (*corona*)	5. a joining together; in grammar, a word used to connect words, phrases, clauses, or sentences

Matrimony is an English word meaning *the state of being married.* It is a derivative of the Latin word ________________________ . This Latin word comes from *another* Latin word we studied earlier. Can you guess the word? ____

D. PRONOUN CHANTS

Study the new chant below. It is in two parts and we will chant from top to bottom instead of across. Basic meanings are given but you are not required to know them.

Saxum coronam gestat.

PERSONAL PRONOUN CHANT

ego - *I*	nōs - *we*
meī	nostrum
mihi	nōbīs
mē	nōs
mē	nōbīs

↓ ↓

tū - *you*	vōs - *you all*
tuī	vestrum
tibi	vōbīs
tē	vōs
tē	vōbīs

Iulia rosas habet.

Practice writing the new chant below:

E. VERB TRANSLATION PRACTICE

Translate the following verbs. Underline endings.

1. celebrat ______	10. gaudēbimus ______
2. invītābās ______	11. dābō ______
3. amant ______	12. secābat ______
4. lībāmus ______	13. portābis ______
5. celebrābunt ______	14. gaudēbant ______
6. invītābāmus ______	15. dō ______
7. amābit ______	16. secābātis ______
8. lībās ______	17. portābam ______
9. celebrātis ______	18. gaudēbitis ______

F. SENTENCE TRANSLATION

Translate the following sentences. Underline endings and label parts of speech. You do not need to label number 8.

1. Marītus nuptam amat. ______

2. Marītum nupta amat. ______

3. Nupta rōsās portat. ______

4. Familia hospitās et hospitēs* invītat. ______

______

5. Virī et fēminae dōna portant in aedificium. ______

______

6. Marītus et nupta placentam secābunt. ______________________________

____

7. Hospitēs* et hospitae gaudent et celebrant. ______________________________

____

8. Nunc marītus est coniunx et nupta est coniunx! ______________________________

____

*_Hospitēs_ is the plural form of _hospes_ in both the nominative and accusative cases. This word is from a declension we have not studied yet.

G. SAYING OF THE WEEK

Amor vincit omnia (Love conquers all)

Write the saying of the week and its meaning on the lines below.

Saying: ______________________________

Meaning: ______________________________

H. REVIEW WORDS

1. familia — _family_
2. digitus — _finger_
3. ānulus — _ring_
4. dō — _I give_
5. amō — _I love_
6. secō — _I cut_
7. aedificium — _building_
8. lībō — _I sip or taste_
9. portō — _I carry_
10. nunc — _now_

Iulius est hospes et placentam libat.

Unit Five Review - Lessons 23 through 27

A. VOCABULARY (Latin to English)

Study Lists 23-27 for three minutes. Without looking, write the English meanings for as many of the following words as you can remember. Finally, check your answers by looking back through lists 23-27. Use a red pen to write in the correct answers for those you missed or left blank.

1. Gallia ____________________
2. locus ____________________
3. ad ____________________
4. scientia ____________________
5. dēvorō ____________________
6. Deus ____________________
7. vīta ____________________
8. servō ____________________
9. iocus ____________________
10. calcitrō ____________________
11. mātrimōnium ____________________
12. dōnum ____________________
13. celebrō ____________________
14. iter ____________________
15. errō ____________________
16. medicus ____________________
17. infirmus ____________________
18. nōn ____________________
19. mors ____________________
20. crux ____________________
21. pūpa ____________________
22. simulō ____________________
23. mīma ____________________
24. coniunx ____________________
25. hospita ____________________

B. VOCABULARY (English to Latin)

Study Lists 23-27 for three minutes. This time look at the English words first and then look at the Latin. From memory, write as many of the *Latin* words as you can remember. When you are finished, look up the ones you don't remember and write the correct answers using a red pen.

1. Spain ______________________
2. carriage ______________________
3. Britain ______________________
4. poison ______________________
5. sleep ______________________
6. lord, master ______________________
7. I tell ______________________
8. truth ______________________
9. ball ______________________
10. I throw ______________________
11. rose ______________________
12. bride ______________________
13. crown ______________________
14. I ride on horseback ______________________
15. native land ______________________
16. pill ______________________
17. I care for ______________________
18. crutch ______________________
19. church ______________________
20. fault, blame, sin ______________________
21. I laugh, smile ______________________
22. toy ______________________
23. comedian ______________________
24. I rejoice ______________________
25. party, feast ______________________

C. DERIVATIVES

Write a derivative for each of the following Latin words:

1. coniunx ______________________
2. hospita ______________________
3. pūpa ______________________
4. mīma ______________________

5. dominus ______________________ 6. ēvangelium ______________________

7. medicus ______________________ 8. venēnum ______________________

9. locus ______________________ 10. errō ______________________

D. REVIEW CHANTS

Fill in the following chants:

IMPERFECT PASSIVE VERB ENDINGS

-bar	

DEMONSTRATIVE PRONOUN: Singular - this

hic		

DEMONSTRATIVE PRONOUN: Plural - these

hī		

PERSONAL PRONOUN CHANT

ego	nōs

tū	vōs

E. PLURAL NOUNS

Make these nouns plural in the nominative and accusative cases:

	NOMINATIVE	ACCUSATIVE
1. apostolus	__________	__________
2. dōnum	__________	__________
3. pilūla	__________	__________

F. SENTENCE TRANSLATION

Translate the sentences below. Underline endings and label parts of speech.

1. Vir equitat in patriam. ______________________________

2. Puella aegra medicāmentum dēvorābat. ______________________________

3. Iūlius nōn cubābit. ______________________________

4. Hospita invītat marītum et nuptam ad convīvium. ______________________________

____

G. MORE SENTENCE TRANSLATION

Translate these sentences. Label and underline endings as usual. Notice the small changes that occur from one sentence to the next. Number 6 and number 7 are labeled for you.

1. Iūlius calcitrat. ______________________________

2. Iūlius pilam calcitrābat. ______________________________

3. Iūlius pilās calcitrābit. ______________________________

4. Iūlius et Iūlia pilās iactant. ______________________________

____

5. Iūlius et Iūlia nōn iactābant pupās. ______________________________

____

SN Adv LV PrN
6. Iūlia nōn est pūpa. ______________________________

SN LV PrN
7. Iūlia est puella. ______________________________

H. SAYINGS OF THE WEEK

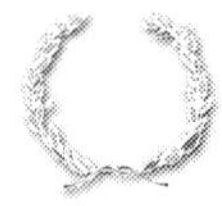

Translate the quotations below:

1. *Errāre hūmānum est* ______________________________

2. *Medice, cūra tē ipsum* ______________________________

______________________________ *(Luke 4:23)*

3. *Ego sum via, et vēritās, et vīta* ______________________________

______________________________ *(John 14:6)*

4. *Rīdē sī sapis* ______________________________

5. *Amor vincit omnia* ______________________________

Lesson Twenty-eight - "Aurea Coma et Trēs Ursī"

A. VOCABULARY

In this lesson you will be translating the story of Goldilocks and the Three Bears. All vocabulary is listed below. New words should be written with meanings three times on a piece of paper. Review the old vocabulary.

Word	Derivative	Translation
1. coma	____________________	*hair of the head*
2. aureus	____________________	*golden*
3. magnus	____________________	*large, big*
4. medius	____________________	*medium, middle-sized*
5. parvus	____________________	*small*
6. dūrus	____________________	*hard*
7. mollis	____________________	*soft*
8. perfectus	____________________	*perfect (just right)*
9. puls	____________________	*porridge*
10. patera	____________________	*bowl*
11. ē, ex	____________________	*out of, from*
12. sed	____________________	*but*

REVIEW VOCABULARY

1. ursus - *bear* (ursa - *female bear*)
2. pater - *father*
3. māter - *mother*
4. infans - *baby*
5. sella - *chair*
6. lectus - *bed*
7. trēs - *three*
8. lībō - *I sip, taste*
9. videō - *I see*
10. sedeō - *I sit*
11. cubō - *I lie down*
12. terreō - *I frighten*
13. dormiō - *I sleep*
14. gelidus - *cold*
15. est - *it is**
16. habitō - *I live in*
17. calidus - *hot*
18. silva - *forest*
19. domus - *house, home*
20. properō - *hurry*

*Although *est* can mean "he is" or "she is", in the story you should use "it is" when no subject noun is named.

B. PREPOSITIONS WITH OBJECTS IN THE ABLATIVE CASE

N.B. Study the prepositional phrases below which will be used in the story.

Notice that when the object of preposition is in the **ablative case**, *in* means "in".

When the object of preposition is in the **accusative case**, *in* means "into".

in silvā - **in** the forest (ablative)
in silvam - **into** the forest (accusative)

in domō - **in** the house (ablative)
in domum - **into** the house (accusative)

in paterā - **in** the bowl (ablative)
in pateram - **into** the bowl (accusative)

in sellā - **in** the chair (ablative)
in sellam - **into** the chair (accusative)

in lectō - **in** the bed (ablative)
in lectum - **into** the bed (accusative)

Quid est?

The preposition *ē, ex* has two forms: *ē* is used before words which begin with a consonant, while *ex* is used before words which begin with a vowel. Objects of preposition which follow *ē, ex* will always be in the ablative case.

ē domō - out of the house
ē silvā - out of the forest
ex ecclēsiā - out of the church

C. STORY TRANSLATION

Translate the story of the Three Bears.
In the story, *Aurea Coma* is the name for "Goldilocks." *Ursus Pater* is "Father Bear," *Ursa Māter* is "Mother Bear," and *Ursus Infans* is "Baby Bear." All verbs are in the present tense.

1. Trēs Ursī habitant domum in silvā. ______________________________

____

2. Ursus Pater magnus est. ______________________________

3. Ursa Māter media est. ______________________________

4. Ursus Infans parvus est. ______________________________

5. Trēs Ursī ambulant in silvam. ______________________________

____

6. Aurea Coma ambulat in domum. ______________________________

____

7. Videt trēs paterās. ______________________________

8. Puls est in paterīs.* ______________________________

9. Aurea Coma pultem** in paterā magnā lībat. ______________________________

____

10. Est calida! ______________________________

11. Lībat pultem in paterā mediā. ______________________________

12. Est gelida! ______________________________

13. Lībat pultem in paterā parvā. ______________________________

14. Est perfecta! ______________________________

15. Aurea Coma videt trēs sellās. ______________________________

____

16. Sedet in sellā magnā. ______________________________

17. Est dūra. ______________________________

18. Sedet in sellā mediā. ______________________________

19. Est mollis. ______________________________

20. Sedet in sellā parvā. ______________________________

21. Est perfecta, sed sella parva frangit.*** ______________________________

____

22. Aurea Coma videt trēs lectōs. ______________________________

____

23. Cubat in lectō magnō. ______________________________

24. Lectus magnus est dūrus! ______________________________

25. Cubat in lectō mediō. ______________________________

26. Lectus medius est mollis! ______________________________

27. Cubat in lectō parvō. ______________________________

28. Lectus parvus est perfectus. ______________________________

29. Aurea Coma dormit. ____________________

30. Trēs Ursī ambulant in domum. ____________________

____

31. Terrent Auream Comam. ____________________

32. Aurea Coma properat ē domo! ____________________

* *Paterīs* is the ablative plural of *patera* (bowl).
** *Pultem* is the accusative singular of *puls* (porrige).
*** *Frangit* means *breaks*.

Est ____________ ____________ Est ____________ ____________ Est ____________ ____________

Lesson Twenty-nine – "Tres Porci Parvi"

A. VOCABULARY

In this lesson you will be translating the story of *The Three Little Pigs*. Memorize the new words below and write them three times with meanings on a piece of paper. Know the review list also.

Word	Derivative	Translation
1. strāmentum	__________	*straw*
2. lignum	__________	*wood*
3. later	__________	*brick*
4. aedificō	__________	*I build*
5. inflō	__________	*I blow into* (used for "huff")
6. anhēlō	__________	*I puff*
7. dēflō	__________	*I blow away*
8. prīmus	__________	*first*
9. secundus	__________	*second*
10. tertius	__________	*third*
11. stultus	__________	*foolish*
12. sapiens	__________	*wise*
13. quoque	__________	*also*
14. tum	__________	*then*
15. diū	__________	*for a long time*
16. dē	__________	*from, out of, about*

REVIEW VOCABULARY

1. porcus	*pig*
2. lupus	*wolf*
3. domus	*house or home*
4. saltō	*I dance*
5. cantō	*I sing*
6. labōrō	*I work*
7. properō	*I hurry, hasten*
8. parvus	*little, small*
9. magnus	*big, large*
10. malus	*bad, evil*
11. trēs	*three*
12. ad	*to, toward*
13. est	*is*
14. et	*and*
15. sed	*but*
16. nōn	*not*

Est primus porcus parvus.

Est secundus porcus parvus.

B. MORE ABOUT PREPOSITIONS WITH OBJECTS IN THE ABLATIVE CASE

Like the Latin prepositions *ē, ex* and *in* (when it means "in" or "on"), the preposition *dē* also takes an object of preposition in the ablative case.

In addition to being prepositions, words like *dē* and *in* can be attached to the front of a verb as a **prefix.**

Identify the two verbs on List 29 which have these prepositions as prefixes and write them on the lines below:

____

____

These two verbs actually contain another word which we have seen before. Can you recognize it? Write this verb and its meaning on the lines.

(word) __________________________ (meaning) __________________________

C. STORY TRANSLATION

Now translate the story of *The Three Little Pigs*. Most of the verbs are in the imperfect tense.

1. Trēs Porcī Parvī domōs aedificābant. ______________________________

____

2. Prīmus porcus parvus domum dē strāmentō aedificābat. ______________________________

____

3. Tum saltābat et cantābat. ______________________________

____

4. Prīmus porcus parvus est stultus. ______________________________

____

5. Secundus porcus parvus domum dē lignō aedificābat. ______________________________

____

6. Tum secundus porcus parvus et prīmus porcus parvus cantābant et saltābant. ______________________________

____

7. Secundus porcus parvus stultus quoque est. ______________________________

____

8. Tertius porcus parvus domum dē latere* aedificābat. ______________________________

____

9. Diū labōrābat. ______________________________

10. Tertius porcus parvus est sapiens. ______________________________

____

11. Magnus malus lupus inflābat et anhēlābat, et domum dē strāmentō dēflābat! ____________________

____

____

12. Prīmus porcus parvus properābat ad domum dē latere. ____________________

____

13. Magnus malus lupus inflābat et anhēlābat, et anhēlābat et inflābat, et domum dē lignō dēflābat! ______

____

____

14. Secundus porcus parvus properābat ad domum dē latere. ____________________

____

15. Magnus malus lupus inflābat et anhēlābat, et inflābat et anhēlābat, et inflābat et anhēlābat, sed nōn dēflābat domum dē latere. ____________________

____

____

16. Trēs Porcī Parvī saltābant et cantābant in domō dē latere! ____________________

____

* *Latere* is the ablative singular form of *later* (brick).

Est tertius porcus parvus.

End of the Year Review - Vocabulary

A. VOCABULARY (Latin to English)

Translate from memory into English as many of the following words as you can. Then look up the ones you are not sure about.

1. līberī ______________________
2. domus ______________________
3. urbs ______________________
4. insula ______________________
5. habeō ______________________
6. glacies ______________________
7. cornū ______________________
8. spirō ______________________
9. ornō ______________________
10. rēgīna ______________________
11. vīnum ______________________
12. locus ______________________
13. narrō ______________________
14. mātrimōnium ______________________
15. sapiens ______________________
16. filius ______________________
17. liber ______________________
18. agricola ______________________
19. videō ______________________
20. lūna ______________________
21. novem ______________________
22. tempus ______________________
23. angelus ______________________
24. nāvigō ______________________
25. fōns ______________________
26. fābula ______________________
27. scientia ______________________
28. iocus ______________________
29. coma ______________________
30. ē, ex ______________________

31. corōna ______________________

32. medicus ______________________

33. caeruleus ______________________

34. herba ______________________

35. gemma ______________________

36. magus ______________________

37. crās ______________________

38. trēs ______________________

39. stella ______________________

40. fēles ______________________

41. rīdeō ______________________

42. errō ______________________

43. secō ______________________

44. imperō ______________________

45. lavō ______________________

46. ōs ______________________

47. dō ______________________

48. fulgur ______________________

49. scopulus ______________________

50. terra ______________________

B. VOCABULARY (English to Latin)

Translate from memory as many of these English words as you can into Latin. Look up the rest.

1. I work ______________________

2. boy student ______________________

3. I love ______________________

4. table ______________________

5. people ______________________

6. tree ______________________

7. fish ______________________

8. cold ______________________

9. plenty, supply ______________________

10. I look at ______________________

11. I live in ______________________

12. mother ______________________

13. I answer ______________________

14. egg ______________________

15. dog ______________________

16. night ______________________

17. I increase ______________________

18. before ______________________

19. head ________
20. clothing ________
21. sword ________
22. bread ________
23. journey ________
24. Holy Bible ________
25. doll ________
26. large, big ________
27. from, out of ________
28. hard ________
29. church ________
30. Germany ________
31. I prepare ________
32. wall ________
33. Jesus ________
34. after ________
35. Christ ________
36. anchor ________
37. grass ________
38. painting ________
39. pill ________
40. fault, blame, sin ________
41. bride ________
42. first ________
43. I build ________
44. ball ________
45. not ________
46. recite, read aloud ________
47. garden ________
48. shoe ________
49. body ________
50. a hundred ________

C. DERIVATIVES

Give derivatives for the following words:

1. salvē ________
2. dormiō ________
3. pater ________
4. tabula ________

5. ambulō ______________________

6. insula ______________________

7. scopulus ______________________

8. glacies ______________________

9. grātīae ______________________

10. corpus ______________________

11. ornō ______________________

12. imperō ______________________

13. tomata ______________________

14. errō ______________________

15. dominus ______________________

16. rōsa ______________________

17. ē, ex ______________________

18. equus ______________________

19. terreō ______________________

20. sōl ______________________

21. decem ______________________

22. punctum ______________________

23. glōria ______________________

24. nauta ______________________

25. floreō ______________________

26. fābula ______________________

27. medicāmentum ______________________

28. theātrum ______________________

29. perfectus ______________________

30. dēflō ______________________

D. MACARONIC STORY

Now write a macaronic story using twenty Latin words from any lists. A *macaronic* story is written in English except for the twenty words you decide to use. You can re-write a familiar story, fairy tale, or fable, or you can write an original story. Feel free to start your story with *olim*, ("once upon a time").

Underline the Latin words used. An example from a familiar fairy tale is given below:

Olim, a puella named Cinderella labōrat for a mala step–māter.

Your story...

You may continue on the back side of this page.

End of the Year Review - Grammar

A. CONJUGATION AND TRANSLATION

Verb Review - Conjugate and translate the first conjugation verb *labōrō* (I work) in the present tense:

PRESENT TENSE

labōrō -	

First conjugation can be called the "___" Family because this vowel appears before most of the verb endings.

Fill in the missing helping verbs which can be used to translate the present tense.

am __________ __________ do __________

Now conjugate and translate the second conjugation verb *habeō* (I have) in the imperfect tense:

IMPERFECT TENSE

habēbam -	

Second conjugation can be called the "___" Family because this vowel appears before most of the verb endings.

Fill in the missing helping verbs for the imperfect tense.

____________ ____________ used to

Conjugate and translate the verb *sedeō* in the future tense.

FUTURE TENSE

sedēbō -	

What conjugation is the verb *sedeō*? ____________

What is the helping verb for the future tense? ____________

B. TRANSLATION

Translate the following verbs. Underline endings.

1. rogābunt ____________
2. lavābam ____________
3. movet ____________
4. dātis ____________
5. spectābis ____________
6. secābāmus ____________

C. NOUN CASES

Write the five noun cases in order: ______________________

____

____

____

____

Which case is used for subject nouns? ______________________

Which case is used for direct objects? ______________________

Which two cases can be used for objects of the preposition? ______________________

____

D. PLURAL NOUNS

Make these nouns plural in the nominative case. Give the meaning of the *plural* form.

Singular	Nominative Plural	Plural Meaning
1. pictūra	______________________	______________________
2. ventus	______________________	______________________
3. saxum	______________________	______________________

Now make the same nouns plural in the *accusative case.* You do not have to give meanings.

Singular	Accusative Plural
1. pictūra	______________________
2. ventus	______________________
3. saxum	______________________

E. TRANSLATION

Translate the following sentences. Underline endings and label parts of speech.

1. Agricola arat. ______________________________

2. Agricola terram arābat. ______________________________

3. Agricolae terram arābunt in agrō.* ______________________________

____

4. Agricola equum spectat. ______________________________

5. Equus properat in stabulum. ______________________________

6. Agricola labōrat in stabulō. ______________________________

7. Equus et porcus errant ē stabulō. ______________________________

____

8. Porcus est magnus. ______________________________

9. Porcus nōn est parvus. ______________________________

10. Iūlia est puella parva. ______________________________

11. Iūlia gallīnās habet. ______________________________

12. Gallīnae stabulum habitant. ______________________________

____

* *Agro* is the ablative form of the word *ager* (field).

ACTIVITY PAGES

Lesson One - Vocabulary Drawing

Draw a picture of the following words from this week's list. Be sure to label your pictures in Latin. *puer, puella, liberi, salve*

A Lesson Two - Word Search

Search the grid and circle the Latin translation of the English words from the list below. Blanks have been provided if you would like to translate first. Words may be spelled forwards, backwards, upwards, downwards or diagonally. An example has been done for you.

T	A	H	P	A	T	E	R	M	R
Q	N	I	T	L	Q	C	S	P	L
W	T	H	L	S	L	U	G	B	A
P	B	X	O	I	I	N	H	N	C
O	Y	R	L	L	F	H	I	F	F
T	O	J	I	V	M	M	L	Y	R
R	M	F	X	Z	E	A	W	Z	A
O	K	R	H	F	D	M	T	X	T
P	A	I	L	I	M	A	F	E	E
R	L	V	L	F	J	N	B	N	R

family *familia*

daughter ______

son ______

brother ______

woman ______

father ______

I carry ______

sister ______

man ______

mother ______

A Lesson Three - Drawing a Roman "Domus"

Draw the following items from a Roman domus. Label in Latin.

kitchen, house, front door, table, floor, ceiling, lamp, dining room, bed, table, chair

A Lesson Four - Crossword Puzzle

Translate the English words into Latin, then match the number of the clue to the numbered boxes going either ACROSS or DOWN.

ACROSS

1 female teacher_______________
3 piece of paper_______________
5 school, game_______________
7 I praise_______________
9 boy student_______________
10 class, classroom_______________
12 good_______________

DOWN

1 bad_______________
2 board, tablet_______________
4 I answer_______________
5 book _______________
6 male teacher_______________
8 girl student_______________
11 I ask _______________

Lesson Five - Drawing a City Scene

Using the road provided, draw the words listed and label them in Latin.

bakery, crowd, money, shop, town

Lesson Six - Macaronic Farmyard Story

A macaronic story is a story where you write in English but use as many Latin words as you can. This type of story is thought to be related to the food, macaroni. Back in history, when everyone in colleges and churches spoke and wrote in Latin, very few of the peasants (common or poor people) could understand what was being said. These priests and scholars began to include words from the local languages within their Latin writing and speaking. This type of "mixed" written form came to be thought of as simple and peasant-like. The peasants frequently ate macaroni noodles and dumplings and the word for *macaroni* became connected with the idea of a story with more than one language in it. No one knows for sure if this is where the name of a macaronic story came from, but it is interesting to study the way words change over time.

Write your own macaronic story below on the space provided. Be sure to use at least ten Latin words. Focus on the words from this lesson by writing about a farmyard. Underline the Latin words you use.

Lesson Unit One Review - Word Search

Search the grid and circle the Latin translation of the English words from the list below. Blanks have been provided if you would like to translate first. Words may be spelled forwards, backwards, upwards, downwards or diagonally. An example has been done for you.

M U I C I F I D E A T M K S F
M U I N I L C I R T P L O K D
K K R L N N X N T L W R M N D
F T L A U D O S K L O U B C M
K V Y H H F E X K R L C M F U
C F H M R D N C V U K V L L R
G T T N I F M R B Q Y Y R S B
C Q Z U A J A A K W L B O U S
P S Q N W L T M P N A M T T N
A K C Q S S L K I T N U S C W
T K M H K U Z I R L R Q A E X
E N L R O J M A V B I N P L X
R H Q E T L H O A T G A K K N
Q Z X U M C A Y D L K M L X L
K L P P Z M N L R M A M O Q R

building *aedificium*
What is it? ______
house, home ______
stable ______
bed ______
boy ______
piece of paper ______
class, classroom ______
I praise ______
crowd ______
I love ______
sister ______
family ______
city ______
shepherd ______
dining room, couch ______
father ______

A Lesson Seven - Vocabulary Drawing

Draw as many pictures from this week's word list as you can. Label your pictures in Latin.

A Lesson Eight - Crossword Puzzle

Translate the English words into Latin, then match the number of the clue to the numbered boxes going either ACROSS or DOWN.

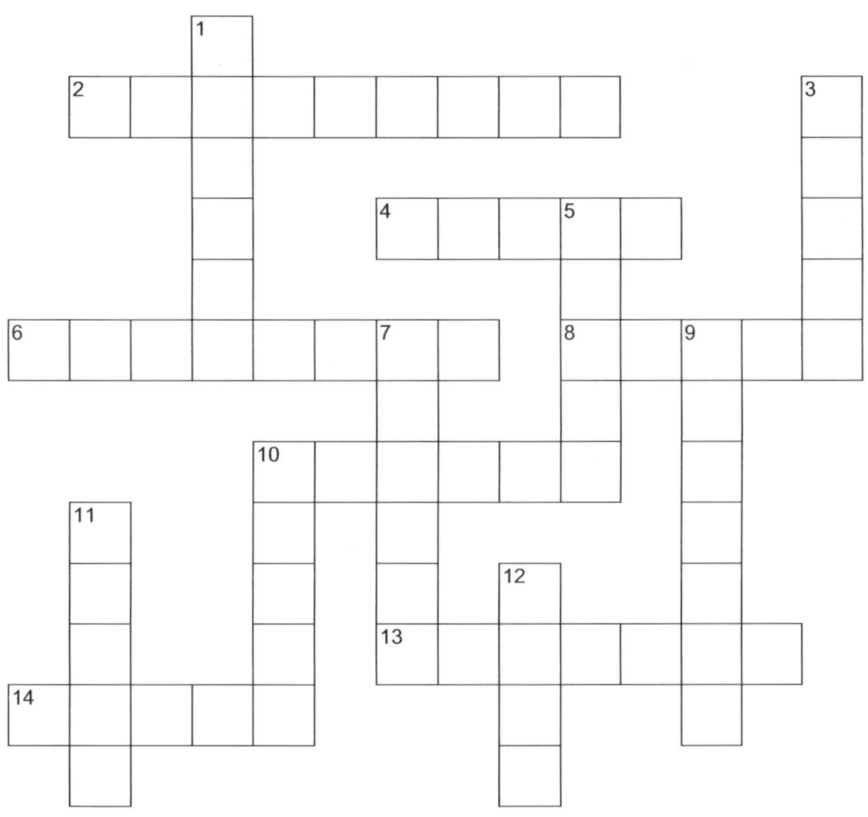

ACROSS

2 rabbit ______________
4 wolf ______________
6 cave ______________
8 bear ______________
10 I frighten ______________
13 pond ______________
14 I see ______________

DOWN

1 animal ______________
3 cat ______________
5 I howl ______________
7 deer ______________
9 squirrel ______________
10 I fear ______________
11 dog ______________
12 frog ______________

Lesson Nine - Sea Creatures & Birds

Color the sea creatures and birds below. Write the Latin name of the animal next to each drawing.

Lesson Ten - The Heavens Worksheet

Color the picture below and label as many items as you can in Latin. Check the reference section on page 299 if you need help.

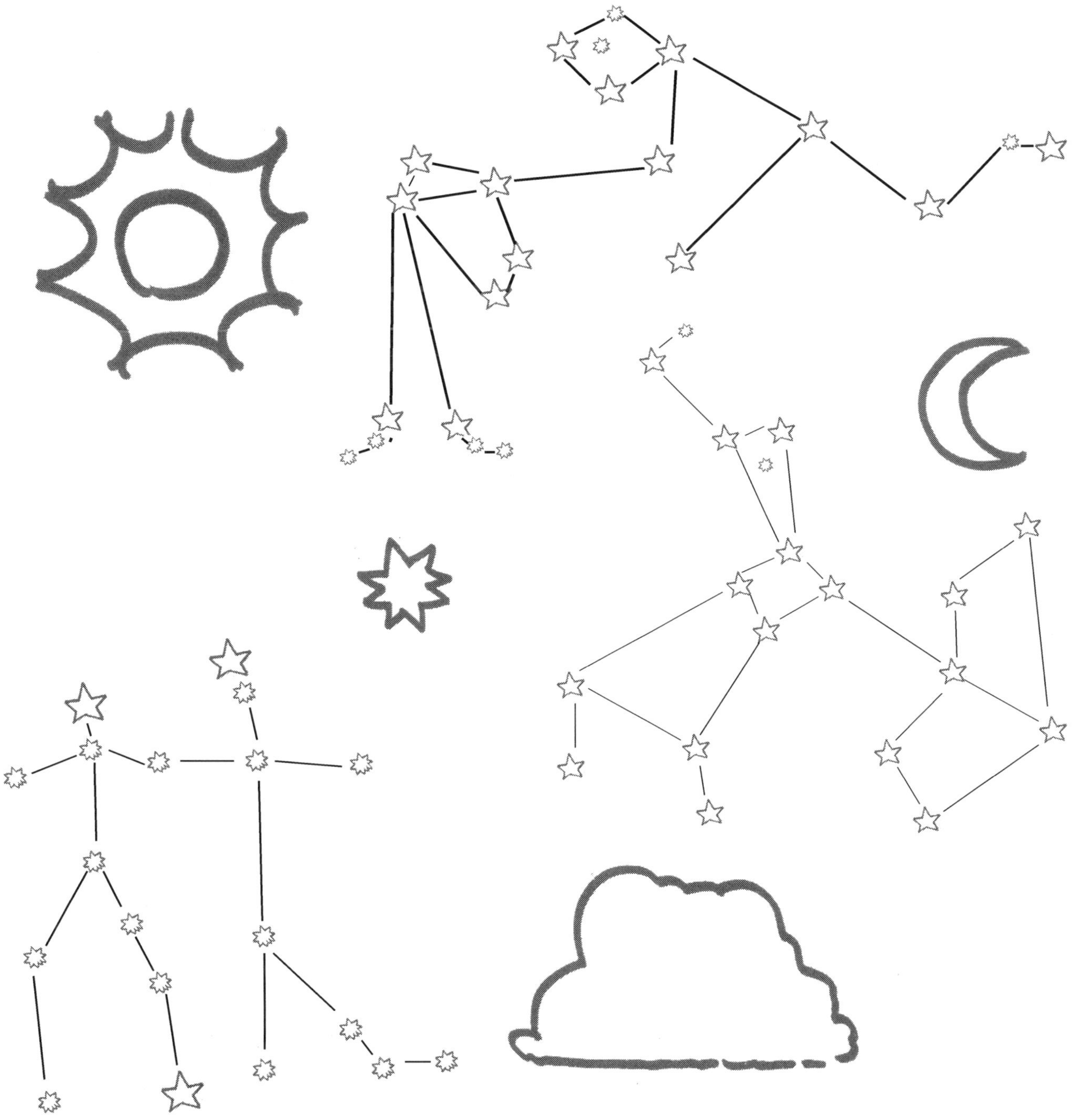

Lesson Eleven - Macaronic Weather Forecast

Write your own macaronic story on the space provided. Be sure to use at least ten Latin words. Focus on the words from this lesson by writing about today's weather and your predictions for tomorrow's weather conditions. Use both the present and the future tenses as you describe and predict the weather. Underline the Latin words you use.

A Unit Two Review - Crossword Puzzle

Translate the English words into Latin, then match the number of the clue to the numbered boxes going either ACROSS or DOWN.

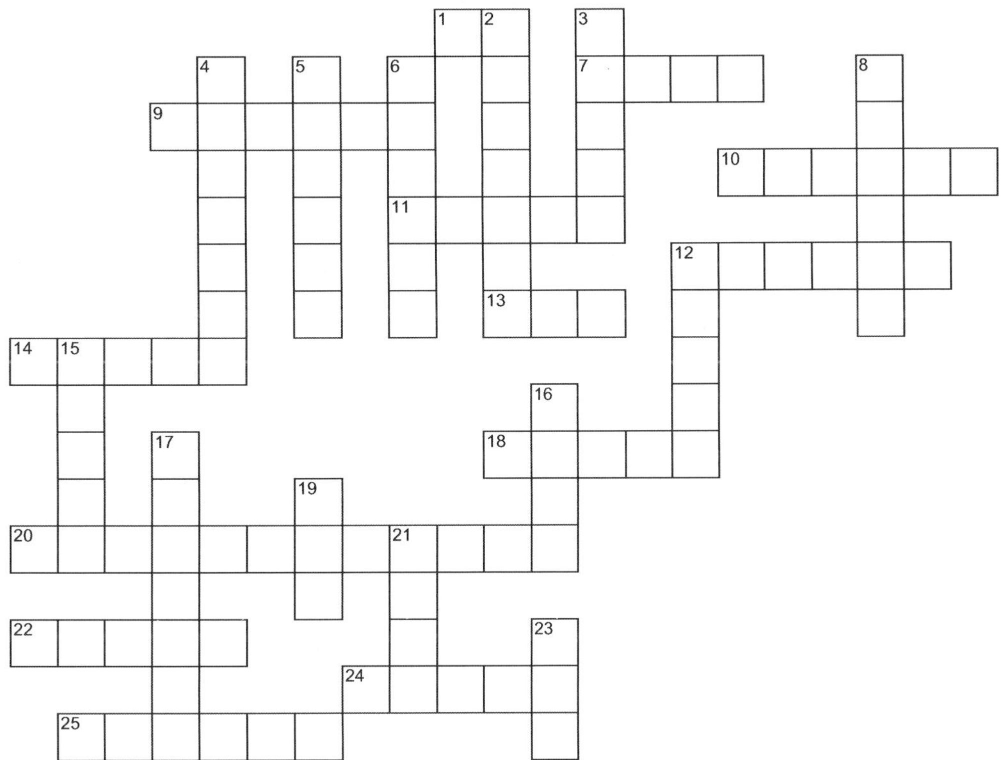

ACROSS

1 I swim ______________
7 moon ______________
9 beach, sand ______________
10 sky, heaven ______________
11 I sing ______________
12 wind ______________
13 sun ______________
14 dog ______________
18 I fear ______________
20 rainbow ______________
22 it's raining ______________
24 I have ______________
25 fish ______________

DOWN

2 ocean ______________
3 I howl ______________
4 hot ______________
5 deer ______________
6 crab ______________
8 lightning ______________
12 I see ______________
15 tree ______________
16 day ______________
17 river ______________
19 wing ______________
21 planet ______________
23 night ______________

A Lesson Twelve - Latin Math

Using the numbers you have just learned, complete the following Latin math problems. Spell out your answers in Latin.

Unus + Tres = ________________

Quattuor + Duo = ____________

Quinque + Quinque = __________

Septem + Duo = ______________

Unus + Unus = _______________

Decem - Duo = _______________

Septem - Quattuor = ___________

Tres + Quinque = _____________

Octo - Sex = _________________

Novem + Unus = ______________

Challenge Multiplication Questions!

Decem x Decem = ____________

Decem x Centum = ___________

(More math on the back of this page)

Roman Numerals

Now write Roman numerals 1-10 in order on the blanks provided below.

Choose from the following:

IX, VII, I, X, III, V, II, IV, VIII, VI

1. ________________
2. ________________
3. ________________
4. ________________
5. ________________
6. ________________
7. ________________
8. ________________
9. ________________
10. ________________

Lesson Thirteen - Macaronic Thanksgiving Story

Write your own macaronic story below on the space provided. Use at least ten Latin words. Focus on words from this lesson by writing about a favorite Thanksgiving memory. Underline the Latin words you use.

A Lesson Fourteen - Anagrams

For this activity you will have to unscramble the English words and translate them into Latin. Write the English words in the first column of blanks and then write the Latin translation in the second column. Choose your favorite and draw a picture at the bottom of the page.

	English	Latin
yirruh (2 words)	______ ______________________	______________________
eefbor	______________________	______________________
tinemu	______________________	______________________
dlasuin	______________________	______________________
onno	______________________	______________________
mite	______________________	______________________
yotad	______________________	______________________
onw	______________________	______________________

Lesson Fifteen - Labeling the Body in Latin

Label the following body parts in Latin: *eye, leg, arm, foot, ear, nose, hand, tooth, finger, heart*

Lesson Sixteen - Christmas Acrostic Poem

Using the letters from the word *Christmas* in English, write an acrostic poem with any Latin vocabulary you can think of. An **acrostic poem** is a kind of poem where each word you use has to start with the letter of the word you have spelled downwards. In this poem, your words should all have something to do with Christmas. The first line has been written for you.

When you finish, you may color in the nativity scene back in the lesson pages.

C HRISTUS

H ____________________

R ____________________

I ____________________

S ____________________

T ____________________

M ____________________

A ____________________

S ____________________

A Lesson Seventeen - Drawing Clothing

Using words from this week's vocabulary list, dress either Julius or Julia. Label the clothing you draw in Latin.

Word List

green *viridis*
arm ______
four ______
birthday ______
toga ______
eye ______
number ______
minute ______
body ______
time ______
today ______
angel ______
ring ______
boot ______
please ______
thanks ______
one ______
you're welcome ______

A Unit Three Review - Word Search

Search the grid and circle the Latin translation of the English words on the previous page. Blanks have been provided if you would like to translate first. Words may be spelled forwards, backwards, upwards, downwards or diagonally. An example has been done for you.

V	L	Y	F	C	Z	E	K	C	O	R	P	U	S	C	K
N	O	N	T	Q	V	I	N	L	X	N	H	K	J	F	G
G	T	C	Y	T	X	D	I	Q	U	A	T	T	U	O	R
S	R	M	U	W	R	O	H	A	V	H	J	W	H	T	M
R	U	A	M	L	M	H	I	G	K	B	R	D	D	U	Q
S	Z	P	T	F	U	B	L	O	R	K	I	T	I	Z	Q
V	U	Q	M	I	Y	S	E	T	T	E	Q	H	A	S	K
I	H	L	R	E	A	J	S	K	S	Q	C	G	I	S	Q
R	X	S	U	X	T	E	T	N	T	C	I	P	U	F	L
I	K	U	M	N	G	H	A	L	A	L	L	R	Y	J	W
D	N	N	Q	W	A	T	T	R	A	A	E	Y	G	Z	X
I	M	U	N	G	A	B	B	C	C	M	F	Z	J	N	M
S	K	D	Y	L	C	M	K	E	U	T	T	L	M	L	L
C	W	K	I	M	Q	V	T	N	R	P	T	T	L	Y	L
M	K	S	N	R	F	P	S	U	L	E	G	N	A	T	M
J	M	U	T	C	N	U	P	L	K	R	R	M	J	Y	R

Lesson Eighteen - Macaronic Sea Adventure Story

Write your own macaronic story below on the space provided. Be sure to use at least ten Latin words. Focus on the words from this lesson by writing about an adventure at sea. Underline the Latin words you use.

Lesson Nineteen - Comic Strip

Using the squares provided, draw a macaronic-style comic strip using at least five Latin words from List 19.

A Lesson Twenty - Crossword Puzzle

Translate the English words into Latin, then match the number of the clue to the numbered boxes going either ACROSS or DOWN.

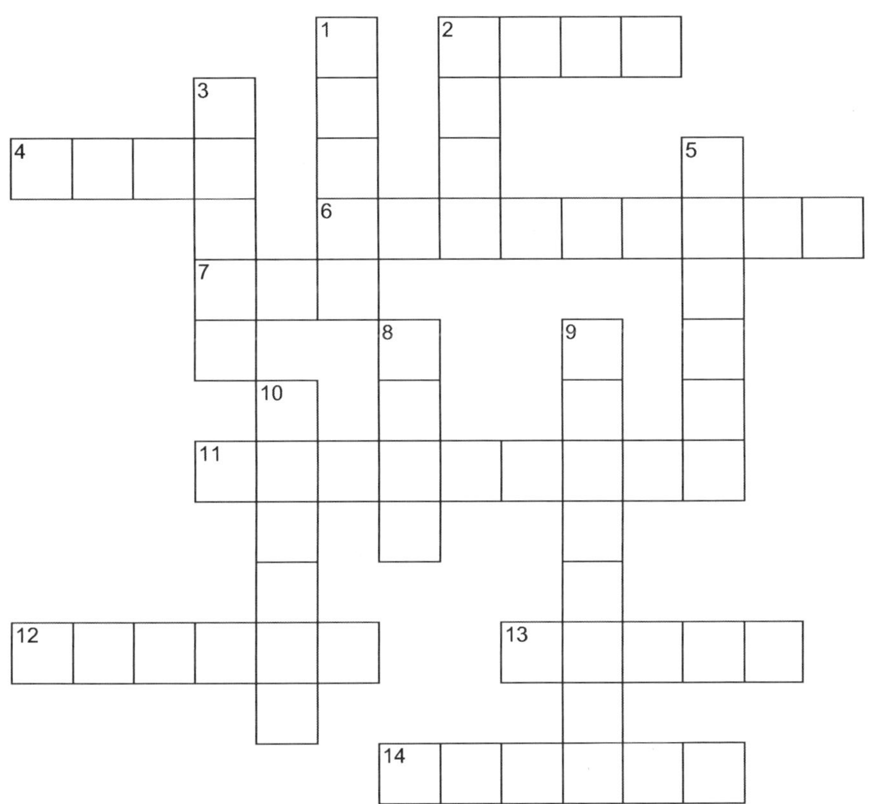

ACROSS

2 flower
4 shovel
6 insects
7 grape
11 we dig
12 leaf
13 vineyard
14 grass

DOWN

1 plant
2 fountain
3 apple
5 you bloom, flourish
8 bee
9 orchard
10 garden

Lesson Twenty-One - Drawing Food on a Plate

Decide if you will be serving ***ientaculum, pradium,*** or ***cena***. Draw and label in Latin the food you would serve. You may also decorate the table.

A Lesson Twenty-two - Macaronic Poem

Write a macaronic poem. Use at least five Latin words from List 22. You may also use words from other lists if you'd like.

Crossword Clues

ACROSS

1 plant
2 pirate
4 arrow
7 carrots
10 I paint
11 poem, song
14 paintbrushes
17 walls
18 story
21 shore
22 bread
23 soldier
24 flower
25 we fight

DOWN

1 spears
2 painter
3 king
5 you steer
6 they listen
8 lunch
9 we dig
12 we sail
13 cookies (little cakes)
15 food
16 you taste
19 sea
20 sails, curtains

A Unit Four Review - Crossword Puzzle

Translate the English words into Latin, then match the number of the clue to the numbered boxes going either ACROSS or DOWN.

Lesson Twenty-three - Roman Empire Map

Using the map of the Roman Empire below, color the *terra* and the *mare*. Then label Germany, France, Rome, Spain, Italy, and Britain in Latin. If you have extra time, you may draw some modes of transportation (*carruca, navis,* or other things).

1. ______________________________
2. ______________________________
3. ______________________________
4. ______________________________
5. ______________________________

☆ ______________________________

Lesson Twenty-four - Comic Strip

Using the squares provided, draw a macaronic-style comic strip using at least five Latin words from List 24.

A Lesson Twenty-five - Anagrams

For this activity you will have to unscramble the English words and translate them into Latin. Write the English words in the first column of blanks and then write the Latin translation in the second column. Choose your favorite and draw a picture at the bottom of the page.

	English	Latin
sorcs	__________	__________
llyBHbeoi (2 words)	__________	__________
bomt	__________	__________
ahdte	__________	__________
lwrod	__________	__________
soodngew (2 words)	__________	__________
sopltea	__________	__________
tthru	__________	__________

A Lesson Twenty-six - Birthday Party!

Julia and Julius are throwing a birthday party for Saxum. Color in the picture and draw a word from this week's list as the present you would give.

Lesson Twenty-seven - Macaronic Wedding Story

Write your own macaronic story below on the space provided. Be sure to use as many Latin words as you can. Focus on the words from this lesson by writing about a wedding.

Word List

apostle *apostolus*	comedian ______
carriage ______	party, feast ______
Spain ______	hostess ______
pill ______	crown ______
tomb ______	I pretend ______
medicine ______	church ______
toy ______	knowledge ______

Unit Five Review - Word Search

Search the gird and circle the Latin translation of the words from the list below. Words may be spelled forwards, backwards, up, down or diagonally. An example has been done for you.

V	C	A	R	R	U	C	A	M	H	V	G	Q	K
B	M	U	R	H	C	L	U	P	E	S	Z	X	K
M	C	K	B	L	D	J	Y	C	J	G	Y	F	H
E	O	K	P	D	T	L	O	T	M	F	V	L	K
D	N	M	A	C	S	R	L	U	R	M	T	W	S
I	V	C	R	I	O	I	I	R	U	X	P	A	U
C	I	T	S	N	S	R	M	R	L	I	F	I	L
A	V	N	A	C	B	E	T	U	L	T	H	N	O
M	I	N	Q	I	I	S	L	U	L	Z	D	A	T
E	U	L	D	F	A	E	L	C	M	O	W	P	S
N	M	U	X	L	L	A	N	T	C	L	Q	S	O
T	L	B	P	B	M	X	K	T	K	E	J	I	P
U	C	A	T	I	P	S	O	H	I	Q	J	H	A
M	C	O	M	O	E	D	U	S	C	A	M	X	L

A Lesson Twenty-eight - Illustrate "Aurea Coma et Tres Ursi"

Illustrate the story of *Aurea Coma et Tres Ursi*. You do not need to label your drawing.

A Lesson Twenty-nine - Illustrate "Tres Porci Parvi"

Illustrate the story of *Tres Porci Parvi.* You do not need to label your drawing.

Word List

blue *caeruleus*	button ______
cat ______	front door ______
wise man ______	sleep ______
soft ______	good ______
Who is it? ______	river ______
jewel ______	orchard ______
night ______	anchor ______
seat, chair ______	noon ______
I order ______	five ______
small ______	cook ______
lord, master ______	I kill ______
I invite ______	cliff, rock formation ______
ear ______	breakfast ______

Vocabulary Review - Word Search

Search the gird and circle the Latin translation of the English word from the list on the previous page. Words may be spelled forwards, backwards, upwards, downwards or diagonally. An example has been done for you.

T	T	J	O	K	B	Y	O	T	I	V	N	I	X	M	H	V	T
W	E	F	R	N	X	Q	S	S	M	A	G	U	S	G	K	T	G
W	M	G	E	O	L	P	R	E	M	L	S	U	U	Q	O	C	Y
M	P	L	P	S	C	K	L	S	I	X	N	O	X	N	R	R	L
W	E	O	M	I	Z	E	R	I	N	D	K	L	V	D	R	Z	I
F	S	B	I	R	V	K	N	U	T	S	I	S	E	L	E	F	L
X	T	U	M	U	K	M	Q	Q	U	S	F	R	M	M	L	Y	O
I	A	L	K	A	U	U	S	L	S	D	T	U	E	P	M	I	I
R	S	U	R	I	I	D	U	O	O	U	I	Y	Y	M	T	F	E
T	M	S	T	N	T	P	L	M	M	R	V	T	L	A	Z	P	N
S	K	S	Q	O	O	U	I	R	A	N	A	R	C	U	T	N	T
D	O	U	F	C	N	N	N	M	N	N	U	I	A	F	S	S	A
M	E	K	S	B	U	I	O	I	C	C	L	S	L	P	R	I	C
K	K	R	R	S	O	P	T	O	C	P	F	U	B	C	B	L	U
X	S	E	L	L	A	E	R	R	P	A	V	L	O	K	M	L	L
A	M	M	E	G	J	A	D	U	U	I	N	L	N	G	K	O	U
S	U	T	L	U	T	S	S	I	U	S	R	W	U	D	B	M	M
C	A	E	R	U	L	E	U	S	V	K	M	Y	S	M	Y	V	K

ACROSS

4 she breathes
7 queen
8 we will tell
10 you all hurry
13 nine
14 gardens
17 we steer
18 tomorrow
20 dolphin
23 crowns
26 hand
28 baby
32 boots
33 she reads aloud
36 Spain
38 hen
42 I swim
43 school, game
44 entrance room
45 I wash
47 carraiges
49 I sleep
50 but
51 he will help
52 he will praise
53 Who is it?
55 foolish
56 yellow
57 I fly
58 rocks

DOWN

1 they were seeing
2 family, household
3 What is it?
5 manger
6 I rejoice
9 also
11 noon
12 theater
15 raft
16 we are dancing
19 sleep
21 stars
22 village
23 rabbits
24 he digs
25 bread
27 daughter
29 hot
30 he will kill
31 I was preparing
34 you all were working
35 we walk
37 thanksgiving
39 I will shine
40 bowl
41 you all increase
46 truth
48 wind
54 I give

Grammar Review - Crossword Puzzle

Translate the English words into Latin, then match the number of the clue to the numbered boxes going either ACROSS or DOWN. You may work with a partner.

REFERENCE PAGES

A Note About Chants

Learn all the chants in the order they appear on the page – starting with the far left column and moving down the page; then back to the top of the second column, and so forth.

Remember that classical education follows the Trivium and this is a grammar-level curriculum. In the grammar stage students memorize and chant many things that they might not understand completely, but as they progress through the Logos Latin series they will build on this knowledge.

Verb Chants

FIRST CONJUGATION

amō	amāmus
amās	amātis
amat	amant

SECOND CONJUGATION

videō	vidēmus
vidēs	vidētis
videt	vident

LINKING VERB (PRESENT TENSE)

sum	sumus
es	estis
est	sunt

POSSUM CHANT

possum	possumus
potes	potestis
potest	possunt

PRESENT TENSE VERB ENDINGS

-ō	-mus
-s	-tis
-t	-nt

FUTURE TENSE VERB ENDINGS

-bō	-bimus
-bis	-bitis
-bit	-bunt

IMPERFECT TENSE VERB ENDINGS

-bam	-bāmus
-bās	-bātis
-bat	-bant

PERFECT TENSE VERB ENDINGS

-ī	-imus
-istī	-istis
-it	-ērunt

FUTURE PERFECT TENSE VERB ENDINGS

-erō	-erimus
-eris	-eritis
-erit	-erint

PLUPERFECT TENSE VERB ENDINGS

-eram	-erāmus
-erās	-erātis
-erat	-erant

Verb Chants (continued)

PRESENT PASSIVE VERB ENDINGS

-r	-mur
-ris	-minī
-tur	-ntur

FUTURE PASSIVE VERB ENDINGS

-bor	-bimur
-beris	-biminī
-bitur	-buntur

IMPERFECT PASSIVE VERB ENDINGS

-bar	-bamur
-baris	-baminī
-batur	-bantur

Noun Chants

Noun chant endings do not have meanings in the same way that verb endings do. Instead, noun endings can tell what part of speech a word is, such as the subject noun. Like verbs, nouns have different families which are called *declensions.*

FIRST DECLENSION

-a	-ae
-ae	-ārum
-ae	-īs
-am	-ās
-ā	-īs

SECOND DECLENSION

-us	-ī
-ī	-ōrum
-ō	-īs
-um	-ōs
-ō	-īs

SECOND DECLENSION NEUTER

-um	-a
-ī	-ōrum
-ō	-īs
-um	-a
-ō	-īs

DEMONSTRATIVE PRONOUNS

(memorize these two charts across, not down)

SINGULAR - THIS

→ → →

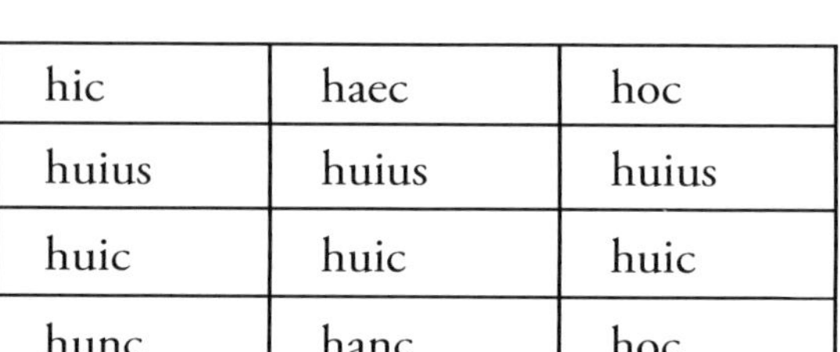

hic	haec	hoc
huius	huius	huius
huic	huic	huic
hunc	hanc	hoc
hōc	hāc	hōc

PLURAL - THESE

→ → →

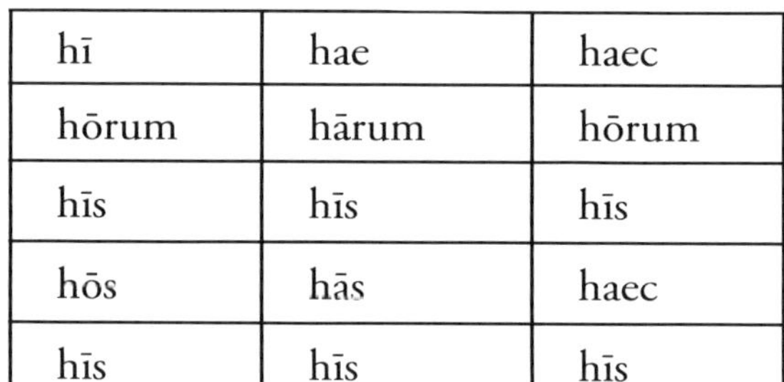

hī	hae	haec
hōrum	hārum	hōrum
hīs	hīs	hīs
hōs	hās	haec
hīs	hīs	hīs

Noun Chants (continued)

PERSONAL PRONOUNS

1. SINGULAR - FIRST PERSON (I/ME)

ego
meī
mihi
mē
mē

2. SINGULAR - SECOND PERSON (YOU)

tū
tuī
tibi
tē
tē

3. PLURAL - FIRST PERSON (WE)

nōs
nostrum
nōbis
nōs
nōbīs

4. PLURAL - SECOND PERSON (YOU ALL)

vōs
vestrum
vōbīs
vōs
vōbīs

S Sayings of the Week

Here is a list of all the Sayings of the Week:

1. *Fide et amore* (By faith and love)
2. *Vir sapit qui pauca loquitur* (Wise is the man who talks little)
3. *Festina lente* (Make haste slowly)
4. *Ex libris* (From the books of)
5. *Vox populi* (The voice of the people)
6. *Labor omnia vincit* (Work conquers all)
7. *Montani semper liberi* (Mountaineers are always free)
8. *Cave canem* (Beware of the dog)
9. *Piscem natare docere* (To teach a fish to swim)
10. *Sol lucet omnibus* (The sun shines on all)
11. *In principio creavit Deus caelum et terram* (In the beginning God created the heavens and the earth)
12. *E pluribus unum* (One out of many)
13. *Date, et dabitur vobis* (Give, and it shall be given to you)
14. *Tempus fugit* (Time flies)
15. *Dum spiro, spero* (While I breathe, I hope)
16. *Gloria in excelsis Deo* (Glory to God in the highest)
17. *Ante Christum natus* (Before Christ's birth)
18. *Nota bene* (Note Well)
19. *Pax potior bello* (Peace is more powerful than war)
20. *Fructu non foliis arborem aestima* (Judge a tree by its fruit, not by its leaves)
21. *Panem et circenses* (Bread and circuses)
22. *Poeta nasquitur, non fit* (A poet is born, not made)
23. *Errare humanum est* (To err is human)
24. *Medice, cura te ipsum* (Physician, heal thyself)
25. *Ego sum via, et veritas, et vita* (I am the Way, the Truth, and the Life)
26. *Ride si sapis* (Laugh, if you are wise)
27. *Amor vincit omnia* (Love conquers all)

Constellation Map

Aquarius (water carrier)

Geminus (twins)

Sagittarius (archer)

Scorpion (scorpius)

Libra (scales)

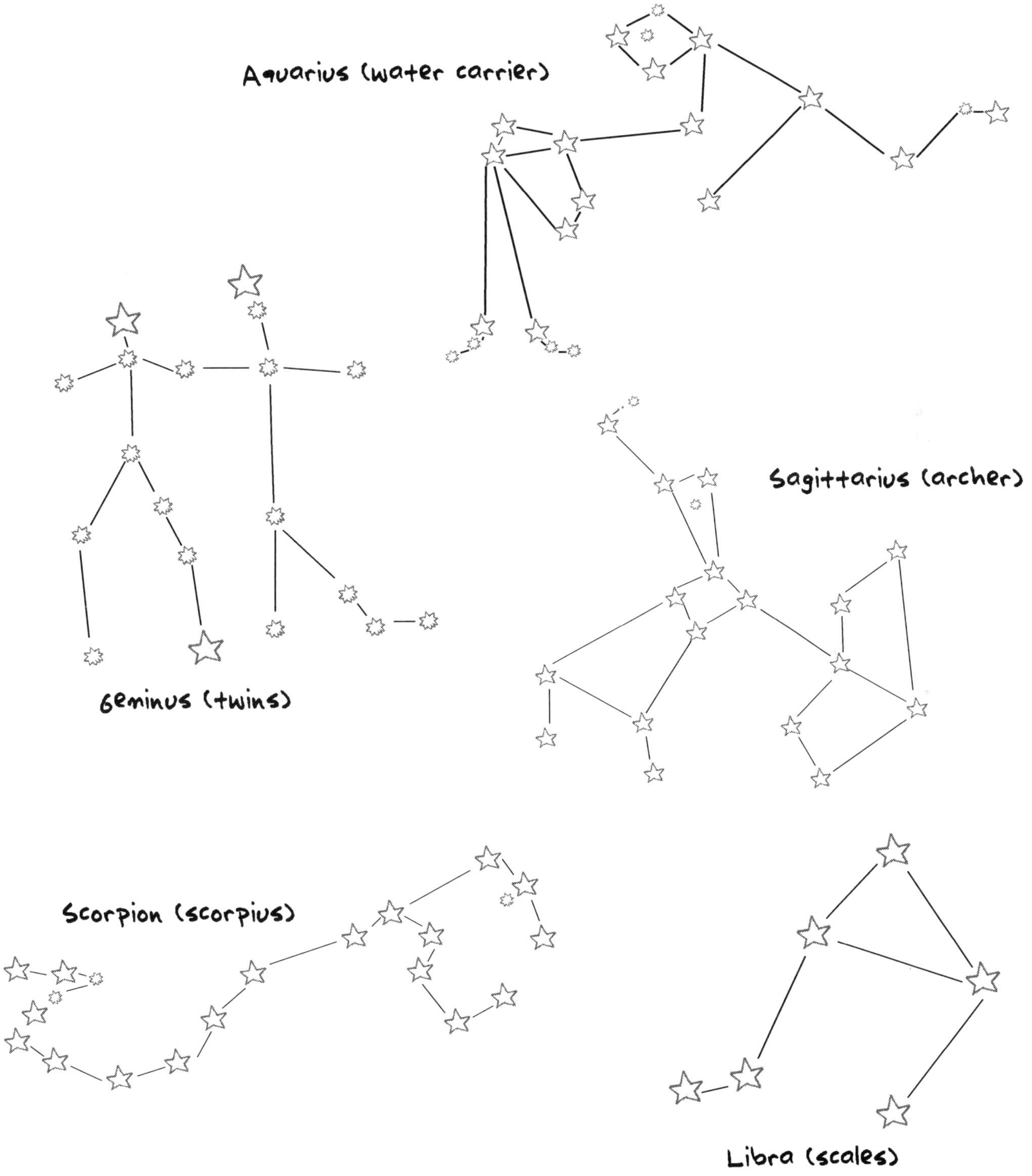

Glossary: Latin to English

The number after the word indicates in which lesson the word was introduced.

A

ad (23)	*to, toward*
aedificō (29)	*I build*
aedificium (5)	*building*
aeger (24)	*sick*
āēr (7)	*air*
ager (6)	*field*
agricola (6)	*farmer*
āla (9)	*wing*
ambulō (5)	*I walk*
amō (1)	*I love*
ancora (18)	*anchor*
angelus (16)	*angel*
anhēlō (29)	*I puff*
animal (8)	*animal*
annus (14)	*year*
ante (14)	*before*
ānulus (17)	*ring*
apis (20)	*bee*
apostolus (25)	*apostle*
aqua (7)	*water*
aquārius (10)	*water-carrier*
aquila (9)	*eagle*
arbor (7)	*tree*
arcus pluvius (11)	*rainbow*
armilla (17)	*bracelet*
arō (6)	*I plow*
asinus (16)	*donkey*
astrum (10)	*constellation*
ātrium (3)	*entrance room*
augeō (12)	*I increase*
aureus (28)	*golden*
auris (15)	*ear*
aurum (18)	*gold*
auscultō (22)	*I listen to*
avia (13)	*grandmother*
avis (9)	*bird*
avus (13)	*grandfather*

B

baculum (24)	*crutch*
bellum (19)	*war*
bestiola (20)	*insect*
Biblia Sacra (25)	*Holy Bible*
bonus (4)	*good*
bōs (6)	*cow, bull*
brācae (17)	*pants*
brācchium (15)	*arm*
Britānnia (23)	*Britain*
būbula (21)	*beef*

C

caelum (10)	*sky, heaven*
caeruleus (22)	*blue*
calceus (17)	*shoe, slipper*
calcitrō (26)	*I kick*
calidus (11)	*hot*
caliga (17)	*boot*
campus (7)	*plain, level area*
cancer (9)	*crab*
canis (8)	*dog*
cantō (9)	*I sing*
cantus (22)	*song, piece of music*
caput (15)	*head*
carmen (22)	*poem, song*
carōta (21)	*carrot*
carrūca (23)	*carriage*
cāseus (21)	*cheese*
castellum (19)	*castle*
celebrō (27)	*I celebrate*
cēna (21)	*dinner*
centum (12)	*a hundred*
cervus (8)	*deer*
charta (4)	*piece of paper*
Chrīstus (16)	*Christ*

	cibus (21)	*food*
	cīvis (5)	*citizen*
	columba (9)	*dove, pigeon*
	coma (28)	*hair (of the head)*
	cōmoedus (26)	*comedian*
	coniunx (27)	*husband or wife*
	convīvium (27)	*party, feast*
	cōpia (13)	*plenty, supply*
	coquus (13)	*cook*
	cor (15)	*heart*
	cornū (13)	*horn*
	corōna (27)	*crown, wreath*
	corpus (15)	*body*
	crās (14)	*tomorrow*
	crepundia (26)	*rattle, toy*
	crūs (15)	*leg*
	crustulum (21)	*cookie (little cake)*
	crux (25)	*cross*
	cubiculum (3)	*bedroom*
	cubō (24)	*I lie down*
	culīna (3)	*kitchen*
	culpa (25)	*fault, blame, sin*
	cunīculus (8)	*rabbit*
	cūrō (24)	*I care for*
D	**dē** (29)	*from, out of*
	decem (12)	*ten*
	dēflō (29)	*I blow away*
	delphīnus (9)	*dolphin*
	dens (15)	*tooth*
	Deus (25)	*God*
	dēvorō (24)	*I swallow*
	diēs (10)	*day*
	diēs nātālis (16)	*birthday*
	digitus (15)	*finger*
	discipula (4)	*girl student*
	discipulus (4)	*boy student*
	diū (29)	*for a long time*
	dō (13)	*I give*
	dominus (25)	*lord, master*
	domus (3)	*house, home*
	dōnum (27)	*gift*
	dormiō (3)	*I sleep*
	duo (12)	*two*
	dūrus (28)	*hard*
E	**ē, ex** (28)	*out of, from*
	ecclēsia (25)	*church*
	epulae (13)	*feast*
	equito (23)	*I ride on horseback*
	equus (6)	*horse*
	errō (23)	*I wander, I am mistaken*
	est (1)	*is*
	et (1)	*and*
	ēvangelium (25)	*good news*
	exerceō (15)	*I train, exercise*
	explōrō (7)	*I explore*
F	**fābula** (22)	*story*
	familia (2)	*family, household*
	fēles (8)	*cat*
	fēmina (2)	*woman*
	fīlia (2)	*daughter*
	fīlius (2)	*son*
	flammeum (27)	*bridal veil*
	flāvus (22)	*yellow*
	flō (11)	*I blow*
	floreō (20)	*I bloom, flourish*
	flōs (20)	*flower*
	fluvius (7)	*river*
	fodicō (20)	*I dig*
	folium (20)	*leaf*
	fōns (20)	*fountain*
	forum (5)	*marketplace, public square*
	frāter (2)	*brother*
	fūco (22)	*I color, paint*
	fulgur (11)	*lightning*
	Gallia (23)	*Gaul*
G	**gallīna** (6)	*hen*
	gallus (6)	*rooster*
	gaudeō (27)	*I rejoice*
	gelidus (11)	*cold*
	geminus (10)	*twin*

gemma (18)	*jewel*
Germānia (23)	*Germany*
gestō (17)	*I wear*
glacies (11)	*ice*
gladius (19)	*sword*
globulus (17)	*button*
glōria (16)	*glory*
grāmen (20)	*grass*
grātīae (13)	*thanks*
gubernō (18)	*I steer*

H

habeō (9)	*I have or hold*
habitō (3)	*I live in*
harena (7)	*beach, sand*
hasta (19)	*spear*
herba (20)	*plant*
herī (14)	*yesterday*
Hispānia (23)	*Spain*
hodiē (14)	*today*
hōra (14)	*hour*
hortus (20)	*garden*
hospes (27)	*host, male guest*
hospita (27)	*hostess, female guest*

I

iactō (26)	*I throw*
ientāculum (21)	*breakfast*
Iēsūs (16)	*Jesus*
imber (11)	*rain*
imperō (19)	*I order*
in (23)	*into*
infans (16)	*baby*
infirmus (24)	*weak*
inflō (29)	*I blow into*
inimīcus (19)	*enemy*
insula (7)	*island*
invītō (27)	*I invite*
iocus (26)	*a joke*
Ītalia (23)	*Italy*
iter (23)	*journey*
iuvō (24)	*I help*

L

labōrō (6)	*I work*
lacus (7)	*lake*
lāna (17)	*wool*
later (29)	*brick*
laudō (4)	*I praise*
lavō (17)	*I wash, bathe*
lectus (3)	*bed*
lēgātus (19)	*lieutenant*
liber (4)	*book*
līberī (1)	*children*
lībō (21)	*I sip or taste*
lībra (10)	*pair of scales*
lignum (29)	*wood*
locus (23)	*place*
lūceō (10)	*I shine*
lucerna (3)	*lamp*
lūdibrium (26)	*toy*
lūdus (4)	*school, game*
lūna (10)	*moon*
lupus (8)	*wolf*

M

magister (4)	*male teacher*
magistra (4)	*female teacher*
magnus (28)	*large, big*
magus (16)	*wise man*
mālum (20)	*apple*
malus (4)	*bad*
manus (15)	*hand*
mare (18)	*sea*
marītus (27)	*bridegroom*
māter (2)	*mother*
mātrimōnium (27)	*marriage*
medicāmentum (24)	*medicine*
medicus (24)	*doctor*
medius (28)	*medium, middle-sized*
mensa (3)	*table, desk*
mensis (14)	*month*
merīdiēs (14)	*noon*
mīles (19)	*soldier*
mille (12)	*a thousand*
mīma (26)	*actress*
mollis (28)	*soft*
mōns (7)	*mountain*

	mors (25)	*death*
	moveō (14)	*I move*
	mundus (25)	*world*
	mūrus (19)	*wall*
	mūsica (22)	*music*
	mūsicus (22)	*musician*
	narrō (25)	*I tell*
N	**nāsus** (15)	*nose*
	nauta (18)	*sailor*
	nāvigō (18)	*I sail*
	nāvis (18)	*ship*
	necō (19)	*I kill*
	nīdus (9)	*nest*
	nihil est (13)	*you're welcome*
	nimbus (10)	*storm cloud*
	ningit (11)	*it's snowing*
	nix (11)	*snow*
	nō (7)	*I swim*
	nōn (24)	*not*
	novem (12)	*nine*
	nox (10)	*night*
	nūbes (11)	*cloud*
	numerō (12)	*I count*
	numerus (12)	*number*
	nunc (14)	*now*
	nupta (27)	*bride*
	oceanus (7)	*ocean*
O	**octō** (12)	*eight*
	oculus (15)	*eye*
	oppidum (5)	*town*
	ōra (18)	*shore*
	orca (9)	*whale*
	ornō (17)	*I decorate, equip*
	ōs (15)	*mouth*
	ostium (3)	*front door*
	ovis (6)	*sheep*
	ōvum (6)	*egg*
	pāla (20)	*shovel*
P	**palla** (17)	*cloak*
	pānis (21)	*bread*
	parō (21)	*I prepare*
	parvus (28)	*small*
	pastor (6)	*shepherd*
	pater (2)	*father*
	patera (28)	*bowl*
	patria (23)	*native land*
	pecūnia (5)	*money*
	pēnicullus (22)	*paintbrush*
	perfectus (28)	*perfect (just right)*
	pēs (15)	*foot*
	pictor (22)	*painter*
	pictūra (22)	*painting, picture*
	pigmentum (22)	*paint*
	pila (26)	*ball*
	pilūla (24)	*pill*
	pinna (9)	*feather*
	pīrāta (18)	*pirate*
	piscis (9)	*fish*
	pistrīnum (5)	*bakery*
	placenta (27)	*cake*
	plaustrum (23)	*wagon*
	pluit (11)	*it's raining*
	poēta (22)	*poet*
	pōmārium (20)	*orchard*
	populus (5)	*people, nation*
	porcus (6)	*pig*
	portō (2)	*I carry*
	post (14)	*after*
	praesepe (16)	*manger*
	prandium (21)	*lunch*
	prīmus (29)	*first*
	properō (14)	*I hurry*
	puella (1)	*girl*
	puer (1)	*boy*
	pugnō (19)	*I fight*
	puls (28)	*porridge*
	punctum (14)	*minute*
	pūpa (26)	*doll*
	quattuor (12)	*four*
Q	**Quid est?** (1)	*What is it?*

quinque (12)	*five*
Quis est? (1)	*Who is it?*
quoque (29)	*also*
rāna (8)	*frog*
R ratis (18)	*raft*
recitō (22)	*I recite, read aloud*
rēgīna (19)	*queen*
rēmigo (18)	*I row*
rēmus (18)	*oar*
respondeō (4)	*I answer*
rēx (19)	*king*
rīdeō (26)	*I laugh, smile*
rīdiculus (26)	*funny (as in a situation)*
rogō (4)	*I ask*
Rōma (5)	*Rome*
rōsa (27)	*rose*
ruber (16)	*red*
sagitta (19)	*arrow*
S sagittārius (10)	*archer*
saltō (26)	*I dance*
salvē (1)	*hello*
sapiens (29)	*wise*
saxum (7)	*rock*
schola (4)	*class, classroom*
scientia (24)	*knowledge*
scopulus (9)	*cliff, rock formation*
scorpius (10)	*scorpion*
sciūrus (8)	*squirrel*
secō (21)	*I cut*
secundus (29)	*second*
sed (28)	*but*
sedeō (3)	*I sit*
sella (3)	*seat, chair*
septem (12)	*seven*
sepulchrum (25)	*tomb*
servō (25)	*I save*
sex (12)	*six*
sī placet (13)	*please*
silva (7)	*forest*
simulō (26)	*I pretend*
sōl (10)	*sun*
sōlārīum (14)	*sundial*
solum (3)	*floor*
somnus (24)	*sleep*
soror (2)	*sister*
spectō (5)	*I look at, watch*
spēlunca (8)	*cave*
spirō (15)	*I breathe*
stabulum (6)	*stable*
stagnum (8)	*pond*
stella (10)	*star*
stola (17)	*dress*
strāmentum (29)	*straw*
strix (9)	*owl*
stultus (29)	*foolish*
stylus (4)	*pencil*
sūcus (21)	*juice*
supplicātio (13)	*thanksgiving*
taberna (5)	*shop*
T tabula (4, 23)	*map, board, tablet*
tabula lūsōriae (26)	*a game board*
tectum (3)	*ceiling, roof*
tempestās (11)	*weather, storm*
tempus (14)	*time*
terra (7)	*land, earth*
terreō (8)	*I frighten*
tertius (29)	*third*
theātrum (26)	*theater*
timeō (8)	*I fear*
toga (17)	*toga*
tomata (21)	*tomato*
tonitrus (11)	*thunder*
trēs (12)	*three*
triclīnium (3)	*dining room, couch*
tum (29)	*then*
tunica (17)	*tunic, shirt*
turba (5)	*crowd*
ululō (8)	*I howl*
U umbra (11)	*shadow, shade*
unda (18)	*wave (of the sea)*

ūnus (12)	*one*
urbs (5)	*city*
ursus (8)	*bear*
ūva (20)	*grape*
vaga (10)	*planet*
valē (1)	*goodbye*
valeō (24)	*I am well, strong*
velum (18)	*sail, curtain*
venēnum (24)	*poison*
ventus (11)	*wind*
vēritās (25)	*truth*
vestis (17)	*clothing, garment*
via (5)	*road, way*
vicus (5)	*village*
videō (8)	*I see*
vigilō (6)	*I guard*
villa (6)	*farmhouse*
vīnea (20)	*vineyard*
vīnum (21)	*wine*
vir (2)	*man*
viridis (16)	*green*
vīta (25)	*life*
volō (9)	*I fly*
vulnerō (19)	*I wound*

G Glossary: English to Latin

	English	Latin
A	a hundred	*centum (12)*
	a joke	*iocus (26)*
	a thousand	*mille (12)*
	actress	*mīma (26)*
	after	*post (14)*
	air	*āēr (7)*
	also	*quoque (29)*
	anchor	*ancora (18)*
	and	*et (1)*
	angel	*angelus (16)*
	animal	*animal (8)*
	apostle	*apostolus (25)*
	apple	*mālum (20)*
	archer	*sagittārius (10)*
	arm	*brācchium (15)*
	arrow	*sagitta (19)*
B	baby	*infans (16)*
	bad	*malus (4)*
	bakery	*pistrīnum (5)*
	ball	*pila (26)*
	beach, sand	*harena (7)*
	bear	*ursus (8)*
	bed	*lectus (3)*
	bedroom	*cubiculum (3)*
	bee	*apis (20)*
	beef	*būbula (21)*
	before	*ante (14)*
	bird	*avis (9)*
	birthday	*diēs nātālis (16)*
	blue	*caeruleus (22)*
	board, tablet	*tabula (4)*
	body	*corpus (15)*
	book	*liber (4)*
	boot	*caliga (17)*
	bowl	*patera (28)*
	boy	*puer (1)*
	boy student	*discipulus (4)*
	bracelet	*armilla (17)*
	bread	*pānis (21)*
	breakfast	*ientāculum (21)*
	brick	*later (29)*
	bridal veil	*flammeum (27)*
	bride	*nupta (27)*
	bridegroom	*marītus (27)*
	Britain	*Britānnia (23)*
	brother	*frāter (2)*
	building	*aedificium (5)*
	but	*sed (28)*
	button	*globulus (17)*
C	cake	*placenta (27)*
	carriage	*carrūca (23)*
	carrot	*carōta (21)*
	castle	*castellum (19)*
	cat	*fēles (8)*
	cave	*spēlunca (8)*
	ceiling, roof	*tectum (3)*
	cheese	*cāseus (21)*
	children	*līberī (1)*
	Christ	*Chrīstus (16)*
	church	*ecclēsia (25)*
	citizen	*cīvis (5)*
	city	*urbs (5)*
	class, classroom	*schola (4)*
	cliff, rock formation	*scopulus (9)*
	cloak	*palla (17)*
	clothing, garment	*vestis (17)*
	cloud	*nūbes (11)*
	cold	*gelidus (11)*
	comedian	*cōmoedus (26)*

	constellation	*astrum (10)*
	cook	*coquus (13)*
	cookie (little cake)	*crustulum (21)*
	cow, bull	*bōs (6)*
	crab	*cancer (9)*
	cross	*crux (25)*
	crowd	*turba (5)*
	crown, wreath	*corōna (27)*
	crutch	*baculum (24)*
D	daughter	*fīlia (2)*
	day	*diēs (10)*
	death	*mors (25)*
	deer	*cervus (8)*
	dining room, couch	*triclīnium (3)*
	dinner	*cēna (21)*
	doctor	*medicus (24)*
	dog	*canis (8)*
	doll	*pūpa (26)*
	dolphin	*delphīnus (9)*
	donkey	*asinus (16)*
	dove, pigeon	*columba (9)*
	dress	*stola (17)*
E	eagle	*aquila (9)*
	ear	*auris (15)*
	egg	*ōvum (6)*
	eight	*octō (12)*
	enemy	*inimīcus (19)*
	entrance room	*ātrium (3)*
	eye	*oculus (15)*
F	family, household	*familia (2)*
	farmer	*agricola (6)*
	farmhouse	*villa (6)*
	father	*pater (2)*
	fault, blame, sin	*culpa (25)*
	feast	*epulae (13)*
	feather	*pinna (9)*
	female teacher	*magistra (4)*
	field	*ager (6)*
	finger	*digitus (15)*
	first	*prīmus (29)*

	fish	*piscis (9)*
	five	*quinque (12)*
	floor	*solum (3)*
	flower	*flōs (20)*
	food	*cibus (21)*
	foolish	*stultus (29)*
	foot	*pēs (15)*
	for a long time	*diū (29)*
	forest	*silva (7)*
	fountain	*fōns (20)*
	four	*quattuor (12)*
	frog	*rāna (8)*
	from, out of, concerning	*dē (29)*
	front door	*ostium (3)*
	funny (as in a situation)	*rīdiculus (26)*
G	game board	*tabula lūsōriae (26)*
	garden	*hortus (20)*
	Gaul	*Gallia (23)*
	Germany	*Germānia (23)*
	gift	*dōnum (27)*
	girl	*puella (1)*
	girl student	*discipula (4)*
	glory	*glōria (16)*
	God	*Deus (25)*
	gold	*aurum (18)*
	golden	*aureus (28)*
	good	*bonus (4)*
	good news	*ēvangelium (25)*
	goodbye	*valē (1)*
	grandfather	*avus (13)*
	grandmother	*avia (13)*
	grape	*ūva (20)*
	grass	*grāmen (20)*
	green	*viridis (16)*
H	hair (of the head)	*coma (28)*
	hand	*manus (15)*
	hard	*dūrus (28)*
	head	*caput (15)*

heart	*cor (15)*
hello	*salvē (1)*
hen	*gallīna (6)*
Holy Bible	*Biblia Sacra (25)*
horn	*cornū (13)*
horse	*equus (6)*
host, male guest	*hospes (27)*
hostess, female guest	*hospita (27)*
hot	*calidus (11)*
hour	*hōra (14)*
house, home	*domus (3)*
husband or wife	*coniunx (27)*

I

I am well, strong	*valeō (24)*
I answer	*respondeō (4)*
I ask	*rogō (4)*
I bloom, flourish	*floreō (20)*
I blow	*flō (11)*
I blow away	*dēflō (29)*
I blow into	*inflō (29)*
I breathe	*spirō (15)*
I build	*aedificiō (29)*
I care for	*cūrō (24)*
I carry	*portō (2)*
I celebrate	*celebrō (27)*
I color, paint	*fūco (22)*
I count	*numerō (12)*
I cut	*secō (21)*
I dance	*saltō (26)*
I decorate, equip	*ornō (17)*
I dig	*fodicō (20)*
I explore	*explōrō (7)*
I fear	*timeō (8)*
I fight	*pugnō (19)*
I fly	*volō (9)*
I frighten	*terreō (8)*
I give	*dō (13)*
I guard	*vigilō (6)*
I have or hold	*habeō (9)*
I help	*iuvō (24)*
I howl	*ululō (8)*
I hurry	*properō (14)*
I increase	*augeō (12)*
I invite	*invītō (27)*
I kick	*calcitrō (26)*
I kill	*necō (19)*
I laugh, smile	*rīdeō (26)*
I lie down	*cubō (24)*
I listen to	*auscultō (22)*
I live in	*habitō (3)*
I look at, watch	*spectō (5)*
I love	*amō (1)*
I move	*moveō (14)*
I order	*imperō (19)*
I plow	*arō (6)*
I praise	*laudō (4)*
I prepare	*parō (21)*
I pretend	*simulō (26)*
I puff	*anhēlō (29)*
I recite, read aloud	*recitō (22)*
I rejoice	*gaudeō (27)*
I ride on horseback	*equito (23)*
I row	*rēmigo (18)*
I sail	*nāvigō (18)*
I save	*servō (25)*
I see	*videō (8)*
I shine	*lūceō (10)*
I sing	*cantō (9)*
I sip or taste	*lībō (21)*
I sit	*sedeō (3)*
I sleep	*dormiō (3)*
I steer	*gubernō (18)*
I swallow	*dēvorō (24)*
I swim	*nō (7)*
I tell	*narrō (25)*
I throw	*iactō (26)*
I train, exercise	*exerceō (15)*
I walk	*ambulō (5)*
I wander, I am mistaken	*errō (23)*

	I wash, bathe	*lavō (17)*
	I wear	*gestō (17)*
	I work	*labōrō (6)*
	I wound	*vulnerō (19)*
	ice	*glacies (11)*
	insect	*bestiola (20)*
	into	*in (23)*
	is	*est (1)*
	island	*insula (7)*
	Italy	*Ītalia (23)*
	it's raining	*pluit (11)*
	it's snowing	*ningit (11)*
J	Jesus	*Iēsūs (16)*
	jewel	*gemma (18)*
	journey	*iter (23)*
	juice	*sūcus (21)*
K	king	*rēx (19)*
	kitchen	*culīna (3)*
	knowledge	*scientia (24)*
L	lake	*lacus (7)*
	lamp	*lucerna (3)*
	land, earth	*terra (7)*
	large, big	*magnus (28)*
	leaf	*folium (20)*
	leg	*crūs (15)*
	lieutenant	*lēgātus (19)*
	life	*vīta (25)*
	lightning	*fulgur (11)*
	lord, master	*dominus (25)*
	lunch	*prandium (21)*
M	male teacher	*magister (4)*
	man	*vir (2)*
	manger	*praesepe (16)*
	map	*tabula (23)*
	marketplace, public square	*forum (5)*
	marriage	*mātrimōnium (27)*
	medicine	*medicāmentum (24)*
	medium	*medius (28)*
	minute	*punctum (14)*
	money	*pecūnia (5)*
	month	*mensis (14)*
	moon	*lūna (10)*
	mother	*māter (2)*
	mountain	*mōns (7)*
	mouth	*ōs (15)*
	music	*mūsica (22)*
	musician	*mūsicus (22)*
N	native land	*patria (23)*
	nest	*nīdus (9)*
	night	*nox (10)*
	nine	*novem (12)*
	noon	*merīdiēs (14)*
	nose	*nāsus (15)*
	not	*nōn (24)*
	now	*nunc (14)*
	number	*numerus (12)*
O	oar	*rēmus (18)*
	ocean	*oceanus (7)*
	one	*ūnus (12)*
	orchard	*pōmārium (20)*
	out of, from	*ē, ex (28)*
	owl	*strix (9)*
P	paint	*pigmentum (22)*
	paintbrush	*pēnicullus (22)*
	painter	*pictor (22)*
	painting, picture	*pictūra (22)*
	pair of scales	*lībra (10)*
	pants	*brāccae (17)*
	party, feast	*convīvium (27)*
	pencil	*stylus (4)*
	people, nation	*populus (5)*
	perfect	*perfectus (28)*
	piece of paper	*charta (4)*
	pig	*porcus (6)*
	pill	*pilūla (24)*
	pirate	*pīrāta (18)*
	place	*locus (23)*
	plain, level area	*campus (7)*
	planet	*vaga (10)*

plant	*herba (20)*
please	*sī placet (13)*
plenty, supply	*cōpia (13)*
poem, song	*carmen (22)*
poet	*poēta (22)*
poison	*venēnum (24)*
pond	*stagnum (8)*
porridge	*puls (28)*
prepare	*parō (21)*
Q **queen**	*rēgīna (19)*
R **rabbit**	*cunīculus (8)*
raft	*ratis (18)*
rain	*imber (11)*
rainbow	*arcus pluvius (11)*
rattle, toy	*crepundia (26)*
recite, read aloud	*recito (22)*
red	*ruber (16)*
ring	*ānulus (17)*
river	*fluvius (7)*
road, way	*via (5)*
rock	*saxum (7)*
Rome	*Rōma (5)*
rooster	*gallus (6)*
rose	*rōsa (27)*
S **sail, curtain**	*velum (18)*
sailor	*nauta (18)*
school, game	*lūdus (4)*
scorpion	*scorpius (10)*
sea	*mare (18)*
seat, chair	*sella (3)*
second	*secundus (29)*
seven	*septem (12)*
shadow, shade	*umbra (11)*
sheep	*ovis (6)*
shepherd	*pastor (6)*
ship	*nāvis (18)*
shoe, slipper	*calceus (17)*
shop	*taberna (5)*
shore	*ōra (18)*
shovel	*pāla (20)*
sick	*aeger (24)*
sister	*soror (2)*
six	*sex (12)*
sky, heaven	*caelum (10)*
sleep	*somnus (24)*
small	*parvus (28)*
snow	*nix (11)*
soft	*mollis (28)*
soldier	*mīles (19)*
son	*fīlius (2)*
song, piece of music	*cantus (22)*
Spain	*Hispānia (23)*
spear	*hasta (19)*
squirrel	*sciūrus (8)*
stable	*stabulum (6)*
star	*stella (10)*
storm cloud	*nimbus (10)*
story	*fābula (22)*
straw	*strāmentum (29)*
sun	*sōl (10)*
sundial	*sōlārium (14)*
sword	*gladius (19)*
T **table, desk**	*mensa (3)*
ten	*decem (12)*
thanks	*grātiae (13)*
thanksgiving	*supplicātio (13)*
theater	*theātrum (26)*
then	*tum (29)*
third	*tertius (29)*
three	*trēs (12)*
thunder	*tonitrus (11)*
time	*tempus (14)*
to, toward	*ad (23)*
today	*hodiē (14)*
toga	*toga (17)*
tomato	*tomata (21)*
tomb	*sepulchrum (25)*
tomorrow	*crās (14)*
tooth	*dens (15)*

town — *oppidum (5)*
toy — *lūdibrium (26)*
tree — *arbor (7)*
truth — *vēritās (25)*
tunic, shirt — *tunica (17)*
twin — *geminus (10)*
V **two** — *duo (12)*
village — *vicus (5)*
W **vineyard** — *vīnea (20)*
wagon — *plaustrum (23)*
wall — *mūrus (19)*
war — *bellum (19)*
water — *aqua (7)*
water-carrier — *aquārius (10)*
wave — *unda (18)*
weak — *infirmus (24)*
weather, storm — *tempestās (11)*
whale — *orca (9)*
What is it? — *Quid est? (1)*
Who is it? — *Quis est? (1)*
wind — *ventus (11)*
wine — *vīnum (21)*
wing — *āla (9)*
wise — *sapiens (29)*
wise man — *magus (16)*
wolf — *lupus (8)*
woman — *fēmina (2)*
wood — *lignum (29)*
wool — *lāna (17)*
Y **world** — *mundus (25)*
year — *annus (14)*
yellow — *flāvus (22)*
yesterday — *herī (14)*
you're welcome — *nihil est (13)*